How to be a
SWIMMING TEACHER

The Definitive Guide to Becoming a Successful Swimming Teacher

Fully Illustrated With Practical Exercises

Mark Young

How to be a Swimming Teacher

Note: this book is intended as a course guide and should accompany additional course material as set on an official swimming teaching course by an official Swimming Association.

The right of Mark Young to be identified as the author of this work and has been asserted by him in accordance with the Copyright, Design and Patents Act 1988.

A Catalogue record for this book is available from the British Library
ISBN 978-0-9570031-0-1

Published by: Educate & Learn Publishing, Hertfordshire, UK
enquiries@educateandlearnpublishing.com

Graphics by Mark Young, courtesy of Poser V6.0

Design and typeset by Mark Young and Baines Design, Cuffley, UK

Published in association with swim-teach.com
www.swim-teach.com

Special thanks go to....

- All the children I've taught over the years. Every one of you have helped me to become a better swimming teacher.
- All the children featured in this book – thank you for swimming so well whilst being photographed and allowing me to use your pictures.
- Karen Ellis – for the unenviable task of proofreading.
- Viki – for being an amazing wife and putting up with my endless hours slaving over the laptop.
- Francesca and Carys – for reminding me that there is life outside of work.

This book is dedicated to David Jones.

Thanks for showing me the way.

Contents

Why Learn to Swim?

The benefits gained from learning to swim, especially from a young age, are numerous. Top of the list has to be safety. Swimming pools and open water areas such as lakes and rivers are an attractive source of fun and entertainment and as a result quite often the dangers of water can be overlooked.

The importance for children of learning to swim cannot be underestimated and respect for the water should be taught as early as possible. As children grow and develop, their strength and therefore ability to move around in the water, with or without floatation aids, also increases. This in turn opens up a whole world of fun and enjoyment. This brings us to the next most important reason to learn to swim: fun.

People swim for various reasons. From health and fitness, to escape and de-stress, right up to training and competition. Most of us, particularly children, swim for fun. With fun come health and fitness in the form of exercise and activity – and most swimming pools and leisure facilities are in local areas and are relatively inexpensive.

Ensuring children receive high quality teaching is very important – because learning to swim is a skill for life and the safety aspects of swimming are unquestionable. Having a child taught by a well qualified teacher will ensure they are provided with appropriate skills.

It is important to note, that children should always be supervised around water, regardless of their swimming ability. The most competent of swimmers can get into trouble at any time and in any water environment. Nobody is drown-proof!

Health and Safety

The safety of all pupils in your class is of paramount importance, especially in this day and age, when we can be sued for breathing in the wrong direction!

Ultimate responsibility for health and safety lies with the manager of the pool or leisure facility where your lessons are taking place. That doesn't mean that as a swimming teacher you are not responsible. You are responsible for the health and safety of your colleagues and assistants as well as the pupils you are teaching.

Normal Operating Procedure (NOP)

The NOP for one particular swimming pool will vary from another as some pools are built within leisure complexes, containing many other sports facilities, and some pools are purpose-built. Most pools vary in their depth and size but all pools have their own NOP.

A typical swimming pool NOP should include the following:

- Emergency action plan (EAP)
- Staff responsibilities
- Temperature of water and surrounding air
- Rescue equipment available on poolside and the procedure for its use
- Pool loads: maximum bather load and pupil/teacher ratios
- Staff qualifications

Emergency Action Plan (EAP)

Health and Safety law dictates that businesses employing staff all require an emergency action plan that can be put into use when dealing with all manor of incidents and accidents, however major or minor. Swimming pool EAPs will vary from pool to pool, depending on the NOP.

A typical EAP should include:

- Emergency signal
- Responsibilities of staff members at the time of emergency
- Location of rescue aids
- Procedure for reporting emergencies
- Location of other necessities (telephone, fire escape, first aid kits)

Hygiene

Maintaining a high level of hygiene on the poolside is a matter of establishing some easy habits and regular practices. Very young children in particular need to be watched carefully as they have less control over their bodily functions.

Some basic cleanliness and hygiene checks to consider before the start of the lesson:
- Check that children have used the toilet before getting into the water. This applies especially to younger children.
- Ask if children have blown their nose.
- Long hair should be up inside a swimming cap or tied back.
- Check the cleanliness of the individual and their swimwear. This can be a sensitive issue and therefore has to be approached with discretion.
- Encourage younger children to use the toilet throughout the lesson if they need to. You will have to get an assistant or parent to take them to the toilet if they need to leave the lesson. Be warned though, that there will be children who use a 'toilet break' as an excuse to get out of swimming!

As a teacher you can advise swimmers to refrain from entering the pool and participating in the lesson if you feel they have a condition that puts the health and safety of others in the lesson, the pupil themself or yourself at risk. This has to be done with tact and sensitivity.

Reasons for asking a pupil not to enter the pool could be:
- Open wound
- Cough or cold
- Ear infection
- Contagious disease, e.g. measles etc

There may be many other reasons, conditions and ailments that may cause you to ask a pupil not to enter the pool for a lesson and they are all at the discretion of you, the teacher. It must be stressed, however, that we are swimming teachers, not doctors! We do not have the knowledge, expertise or indeed qualifications to diagnose or advise on any medical condition. The only sound piece of advice you can give, if you feel it is necessary, is that the pupil must go to their doctor for further advice if they have not done so already.

As a swimming teacher, you are a trained professional and represent everything that is associated with the standards expected of a fully qualified, trained professional. Therefore, it is important to set standards and have your own procedures in place. The following need to be considered:

- Check your rescue equipment is in place before pupils enter the poolside.
- Check lifeguard is present, if necessary. Some private pools do not require one.
- Check you are wearing appropriate uniform and the correct footwear.
- Tie back long hair.
- Check the pool area is roped off if necessary.
- Check you have all equipment for the lesson, e.g. floats/toys etc, before the lesson starts.
- Check number of pupils in the lesson. Take a register and recount/check regularly.
- Pupils' own safety checks: long hair, long baggy shorts, jewellery, costume straps, chewing gum.
- Check pupils that need medication have it near by, e.g. inhaler.
- Check pupils are in appropriate depth where possible.
- Monitor pupils throughout lesson for excessive fatigue.
- Discourage unruly behaviour and keep control of the class!

'The art of teaching is the art of assisting discovery.'

Mark Van Doren

What makes a good teacher?

A teacher is looked up to by their pupils as a role model and a source of knowledge and guidance. A teacher possesses several key characteristics that make him or her individual and it is these personal characteristics that can determine a teacher's level of success.

A good swimming teacher requires a wide range of qualities. You will probably be stronger in some areas than others and as you gain experience you will build your competence in all areas.

Teaching Qualities

To be a good teacher and role model to your pupils, you need to possess some essential qualities. These are:

- **Knowledge** – having sound knowledge of your subject gains you respect, not only from your pupils, but from parents and other swimming teachers. You will need to keep your knowledge up to date and always admit when you don't know the answer, but make it your business to find out!

- **Empathy** – teaching swimming requires empathy on all levels. For example, the child who is scared and has every reason to be, the adult who is equally scared or even embarrassed, the child who is over-excited at the prospect of going in the pool and the child who is trying hard but not keeping up with the rest.

- **Patience** – all of the above examples that require empathy will also test your patience. As a teacher you have to accept that not everybody learns at the same rate. Children's behaviour and attention spans will also try your patience at times. Whatever is thrown at you, you must show patience and control at all times.

- **Control and management** – it goes without saying that you must have control over your class, especially with children in a pool. In the classroom at school, children know what is expected of them but this is not always the case in the swimming pool. Children have to be controlled for safety purposes as well as learning purposes. If pupils are being unruly throughout the lesson then not only is the lesson unsafe, but they are not learning anything! The golden rule is to set out your stall early on to show them who is boss. That is not to say that you have to 'rule with fear', otherwise pupils will not want to have swimming lessons with you, just let those that step out of line know they have done so and that it will not be tolerated.

Effective Communication

As a teacher, your job is to pass on information effectively and clearly, and your ability to do this will determine how quickly your pupils learn. Knowledge of your subject is also essential, but how you convey that knowledge is far more important. You could be a world expert on the human body and the scientific principles behind swimming but if you are not able to pass that expertise onto eager-to- learn pupils in a clear and concise way, then you are not a good teacher!

Basic Principles of Effective Communication

- **Positioning** – where you position yourself on the poolside will determine how well your pupils can see and hear you. Study the pool diagrams on page 21 for best practice.

- **Clarity** – passing information on clearly will ensure your pupils do exactly what you want them to.

- **Conciseness** – keep your teaching concise to avoid your pupils becoming confused or taking in the wrong pieces of information.

- **Accuracy** – your teaching has to be accurate as you will be copied, mimicked and quoted, especially by children. Inaccuracy will result in your pupils not learning and in you gaining a reputation as a poor teacher.

- **Enthusiasm** – a sure way to motivate your class and get results is to have an enthusiastic approach. Enthusiasm is infectious and if you are full of it when you teach, your pupils will put every effort into what you ask them to do.

- **Interest** – if the content of what you teach is not interesting then your pupils will not listen and become distracted. Enthusiasm and interesting content go hand in hand, as one breeds the other. The most uninteresting subject can be made interesting with an injection of enthusiasm.

- **Appropriateness** – the teaching points and practices you use will determine the success and outcome of the lesson. If your methods are not appropriate, the pupils do not learn and the lesson becomes pointless.

- **Two-way** – communication works both ways. Ask your pupils questions and listen carefully to those who answer and how they answer. Encourage them to ask you questions at appropriate times.

Motivation

As a teacher you are also a motivator. Some pupils you teach will need more motivation than others. Most children can't wait to get into the pool and start swimming and impress the teacher. You will, however, come across children who have swimming lessons because they have been made to do so by their parents, whether they need them or not. Either way, a motivating teacher brings out the best in pupils.

- **Praise** – this is the easiest, most common form of motivation. Remember to praise effort as well as success.

- **Feedback** – this is a more detailed, constructive form of praise. The pupils are given a clearer picture of how they are performing and improving. If feedback is to be motivational it has to be positive.

  For example, a swimmer returns to the poolside after practicing front crawl leg kick unsuccessfully. Your job is to teach and motivate them. Your feedback should go something like this:

  'Well done, that was a good try' (praise for the effort)
  'You were pointing your toes, which is good, well done.' (positive feedback)
  'Try again, and this time kick your legs from your hips.' (feedback in the form of a teaching point)
  Avoid negative feedback, for example 'Don't bend your legs.'

- **Goal setting** – this is an ideal way of motivating pupils. Setting them a realistic and appropriate goal will encourage progress, and goals come in many forms. Badges and awards are the most common and popular type of goal. The ASA has one of the most comprehensive award schemes in place for swimmers and caters for pupils from beginners right through to advanced levels. It should be noted however that failure to achieve an award or having too much emphasis placed on achieving an award can have the opposite effect. Other types of goals can be in the form of achieving a target time, winning a race or simply moving up a class. Human nature dictates that we are motivated by our perception of our own ability, so it is vitally important that all goals set should be measurable and are achievable in a realistic time scale.

'I hear and I forget
I see and I remember
I do and I understand'
Confucius

'By failing to prepare you are preparing to fail.'

Benjamin Franklin

Planning and Organisation

Prior planning prevents poor performance

The planning of a swimming lesson takes place in advance and helps the teacher to focus on the aims of the lesson ahead. Filling out a simple lesson plan like the one shown over the page takes a minimal amount of time – time that proves invaluable to the outcome of the lesson.

A lesson plan is used as a means of communication. Firstly pre-planning and organisation ensures that the lesson can be conducted safely and effectively. Lesson plans help new or inexperienced swimming teachers to organise exercises and activities for the lesson as well as to gather equipment required prior to the start of the session. This then allows the lesson to flow uninterrupted from one activity to the next in a structured, professional way.

Main areas to organise:
- equipment
- activities
- Pupils

Pupil organisation

This is affected by a number of factors:

- **Teaching area** – the water space available, depth and area of the pool (i.e. near the poolside or lane rope) will all affect the content of the lesson. For example beginners and non-swimmers will not be able to hold the lane rope between exercises, therefore the teacher may have to teach the lesson in the water.

- **Number of pupils** – class size will affect the number of exercises and the amount of time spent on each exercise. Where there are fewer pupils in the class, they can spend more time on the details of each activity. Higher class numbers require the teacher to maintain control and discipline, which makes planning the lesson all the more essential. Oversized classes can seriously compromise safety.

- **Pupil ability** – the aim of the session should always be to improve and progress the pupils' confidence, ability or technique. The ability of the pupils should always be considered when planning the lesson so that the standard can be pitched correctly. If the session is too difficult the pupils will not progress and in some cases even regress, especially in confidence. If the lesson is too easy it will be of no benefit to the pupils and no progress will be made.

Organising a Group

Conducting a lesson with a group of pupils can be done effectively and safely if careful organisation is carried out prior to the lesson. Planning how the pupils will be swimming during the lesson firstly ensures safety and further enhances their progress. Some examples of this type of planning are:

- **Wave swimmers** – the pupils are numbered alternately 'one' or 'two'. Then all number 'one' swimmers are set off on their practice together, followed by the number 'two' swimmers. This method ensures they are all spaced out safely and that the teacher can study each pupils progress more easily.

- **Cannon swimming** – the pupils are set off on their practice one at a time with gaps of 5 – 10 seconds. The teacher is then able to watch each swimmer in turn as they begin and provide feedback either as they swim (if on the back) or when they return or come to a stop.

- **Working with a number of ability groups** – more experienced teachers my be able to work with different ability groups at the same time. The lesson plan my be the same theme for the lesson, but one group of pupils may be able to do more advanced practice than another. If the teacher sets each group off separately, then progress can be monitored. A class like this should split into a maximum of 2 groups and this works best with classes that contain smaller numbers.

Equipment Organisation

All equipment required for the lesson should be gathered in advance and within easy reach on the poolside, ready for distribution to pupils. The numbers of floats, buoyancy aids and toys should be sufficient for the number of pupils in the class and the type of equipment made available should be in accordance with the lesson plan, i.e. relevant to the pupils' ability.

If the teacher is required to teach several lessons in succession without a break, then equipment for all lessons should be gathered and available prior to the first lesson. This ensures the teacher remains on the poolside and in sight of the class at all times.

Activities and Practices

It goes without saying that the practices written in the lesson plan and then used during the lesson should be relevant to both the theme of the lesson and the ability of the pupils.

The chosen practices should be varied so as to prevent boredom for both teacher and pupil and also be planned and organised in a way that tests each pupil's ability, and therefore encourages progression.

Part 2 of this book provides a detailed range of exercises and practices to use when planning a structured lesson.

A lesson plan is a detailed outline of the forthcoming session and is a must for any new up and coming swimming teacher. If the lesson is planned in advance then all exercises and activities can flow from one to the next in a professional way.

An example lesson plan is shown on the next page and typically contains the following information:

- Date and time: the date and time of the planned lesson to be taught.
- Number in class: the number of pupils in the class.
- Pool depth: the depth of the section of the pool the lesson will be taught in.
- Ability: the overall ability of the pupils in the class to be taught.
- Venue: the name of the pool or leisure centre where the lesson will take place.
- Equipment required: all equipment including floats, buoyancy aids and toys that will be needed for all exercises throughout the lesson.
- Aim of the lesson: this can be anything from 'gaining water confidence' to 'improving butterfly technique'. The aim should be relevant to the ability of the class and the teacher's desired outcome.
- Entry: the type of entry into the water used by the pupils. This should be relevant to their ability and confidence levels.
- Warm up: the warm up should be a swim or movement through the water that is well within the class ability level and should last approximately 2—3 minutes.
- Main theme: contains the bulk of the lesson content and should be made up of practices and activities relevant to the aim of the lesson. The main theme should be the longest part of the lesson.
- Contrasting activity: this part can complement the aim and main theme of the lesson or introduce a new activity in preparation for future lessons. Examples of contrasting activities could be sculling, treading water, retrieving an object from the pool floor, star floats or diving (if the depth is safe).
- Exit: pupils can leave the pool via the poolside or the steps.

The list of practices and exercises used in the lesson is also divided into the following:

- Teaching points: these are the actual instructions given to the class, usually verbally, by the teacher to enhance each practice. For example 'point your toes', 'keep your fingers together' or 'kick from your hips'.
- Organisation: how the class will carry out the practice, for example 'all together' or 'one at a time'.
- Duration: the duration of each practice or activity should be estimated and then added up at the bottom to give the total duration of the lesson. This ensures the lesson time is used efficiently and effectively and that classes do not run over time or are not long enough.

Sample Lesson Plan

Date: *1st Aug 08*	Time: *4.00* am/**pm**	No. in Class: *5*	Pool depth: *1.2* m

Ability: (beginners) improvers advanced **Venue:** *Herts Leisure Centre*

Equipment required: (woggles) floats pullbuoy (floaters) (sinkers) fins

Aim of Lesson: *Introduce breaststroke and gain confidence with face submersion*

Practice/Activity	Teaching Points	Organisation	Duration
Entry *Swivel entry*	*Slowly*	*All together*	*30 secs*
Warm Up *2 widths any stroke with woggle*	*Kick continuously*	*All together*	*3 mins*
Main Theme *2 widths full stroke breaststroke with woggle*	*Pull with both hands at the same time*	*All together*	*3 mins*
Static practice seated on poolside	*Kick like a frog*	*All together*	*3 mins*
2 widths supine with woggle	*Turn your feet out*	*One at a time*	*3 mins*
2 widths on the front with a float under each arm	*Kick and glide*	*One at a time*	*3 mins*
2 widths walking using arms	*Keep your fingers together*	*All together*	*3 mins*
2 widths on front with woggle	*Blow your hands forwards*	*One at a time*	*3 mins*
2 widths full stroke with woggle	*Pull, kick and glide*	*All together*	*3 mins*
Contrasting Activity *Prone star float with a woggle*	*Hold your breath*	*All together*	*2 mins*
Pick up a stick held under the water	*Reach for the stick with your eyes open*	*One at a time*	*3 mins*
Exit *Using the pool steps*	*Take your time*	*One at a time*	*30 secs*
		Total Duration:	*30* minutes

Notes

_____
_____
_____
_____
_____
_____
_____
_____

Blank lesson plan templates can be download free of charge from:

http://www.swim-teach.com/how-to-teach-swimming-planning.html

Poolside Positioning

The placement of the teacher on the poolside in front of the class is a crucial part of delivering effective communication. Every pupil in the class must be able to see and hear the teacher at all times and the teacher must have easy sight of all pupils in the water. Below are the two most common poolside positions.

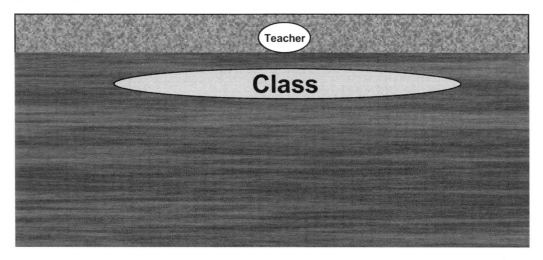

This position is used when teaching from the centre of the poolside

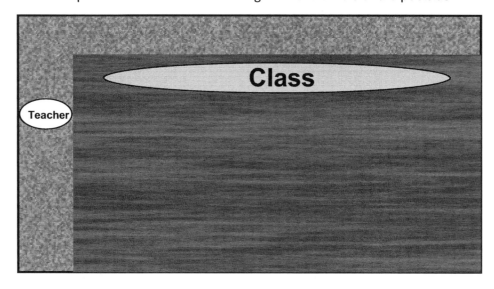

This position is used when the end of the pool is available

The Scientific Principles of Swimming

It is important to understand some of the key scientific principles of swimming as this will provide a greater understanding of how and why strokes are swum in the way that they are.

Floatation

Floating is a characteristic of the human body. Some of us float very well while others do not. It's all down to our relative density. In other words, how dense our body structure is, compared to the density of the water we are attempting to float in. Let us put some actual figures to this:

Freshwater has a density of 1g/cm3
Saltwater has a density of 1.024g/cm3, therefore having a higher density

The average male has a density of 0.98g/cm3 and the average female 0.97g/cm3. We can deduce therefore that most human beings will float to a certain degree, with a small amount of the body staying above the water surface. Females float better than males and both males and females float better in saltwater than in freshwater. Very few adults can float horizontally in the water, yet most children can hold a star float in the horizontal position.

It must be noted that a person's weight has little to do with their density. Muscle is denser and therefore heavier than fat, making fatter people better floaters.
Other factors that effect floatation are:

- The volume of air in the lungs
- An individual's muscle to fat ratio
- The shape of the individual and therefore the location of their centre of gravity

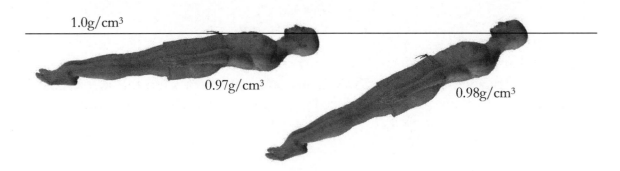

Propulsion

Swimmers have to provide movement in the water in order to propel themselves through it. Types of   movement we use most commonly are paddling, sculling and kicking.

- Paddling is likened to oars on a boat. A large flat surface area pulled in one direction causes another object to move in the opposite direction. In the case of the human body, we pull or push with our hands and arms, causing us to move backwards or forwards in the water accordingly.

- Sculling takes the form of a curved shape in the water made by the hands as they move to find still, undisturbed water. Water that is not moving provides more propulsion than water that has already been moved. All of the swimming strokes require some kind of sculling action. Sculling is the most efficient way of moving our hands and arms through the water.

- Kicking the water with the legs is the least efficient way of moving through the water as it can require a rapid movement that can very quickly become tiring. It can be argued that kicking, be it in an up and down motion or a curved motion as in breaststroke, is another form of paddling or sculling. This is true, but kicking is often the first means of propulsion in the water that children discover and therefore can be classed as a separate form of propulsion.

Resistance

As the body moves through the water, it is met by resistance coming from the water itself. If this resistance is to be easily overcome, the body moving through the water has to be as streamlined as possible. There are three main types of resistance a swimmer will encounter in the water:

- Profile resistance – this is the resistance met head on by the swimmer. As the swimmer moves forward through the water, the profile resistance is pushing him/her back. If profile resistance is to be minimised, the body has to be made as narrow and thin as possible.

- Viscous drag – as a swimmer moves through the water, friction slows him/her down by creating a drag force. As water comes into contact with the skin, forward motion is compromised by the dragging force backwards. Excess body hair and baggy swimming shorts cause large increases in viscous drag.

- Eddy currents – these are caused by an object moving through the water, causing the surrounding water to move and create turbulences. For example, if you place a floating object behind you as you swim, the object will follow you in the eddy current your swimming has created. Eddy currents are generally reduced when profile resistance is improved.

The Non-Swimmer

Non-swimmers arrive on the poolside in all different shapes, sizes and ages.
Some will come with courage and confidence built in, many others will be scared witless! Whatever 'non-swimmers' you are presented with, treat them all the same to begin with by applying a very basic rule – assume they need to be taught everything!

Basics to start with will include:

- Getting into and out of the pool, either via the steps provided or the poolside.
- Moving around in the water, i.e. walking.
- Regaining a standing position from a prone or supine position.

Artificial Aids
Artificial aids should be used as a form of enhancing confidence in the non swimmer. They will also have to be used if the lesson is to be taught in water depth greater than the arm length of the pupils, as a safety measure. The main purpose of artificial aids with non swimmers is to allow them to learn how to propel themselves through the water as soon as they have the confidence to do so.

Types of Artificial Aid
Teachers should fully understand the purpose of any given artificial aid before administering its use. The use of the aid must be appropriate to the needs of the pupil and the teacher must be familiar with how to use it.

Armbands
Advantages:
- Develop early confidence.
- Buoyancy can be reduced as the non-swimmer becomes stronger and more confident.
- Co-ordination can be improved as arms and legs can be used independently.
- Teacher can safely supervise a larger number of pupils in one class.

Disadvantages:
- Pupils can become dependant on armbands.
- They may hinder arm movements, especially in smaller children.

Armbands or Water Wings as they are sometimes called.

Safety rings

Advantages:
- Allow the pupils' faces to be kept clear of the water.
- Support pupils at a higher level in the water.

Disadvantages:
- Can be insecure on some pupils and some children can slip through.
- Can hinder arm action.
- Promote a vertical body position.

Safety Ring

Buoyancy suits

Advantages:
- Can give a high level of support.
- Can promote a horizontal position .
- Allow the face to be kept clear of the water.

Disadvantages
- Pupils may find it difficult to regain the standing position.
- Pupil may be tipped forward too far.

Buoyancy Suit

Floats/Noodle

Advantages:
- Are very versatile.
- Can be used in addition to other aids.
- Can be used instead of other types of aid, therefore encouraging progression.
- Can help gain leg or arm strength when used individually.

Disadvantages:
- Requires a certain degree of strength in the leg kick.
- One arm cannot be used if a float is held.

Noodle

Float

Shallow Water Method

The shallow water method is taught in pools where pupils can support themselves horizontally in the water by placing their hands on the pool floor. Pupils can then add a leg action and then gradually an arm action. Buoyancy aids can be worn if there is a danger of pupils straying into deep water.

Advantages:
- Fast gains in confidence
- Breathing is easy
- Horizontal position is achieved
- May not require any buoyancy aids

Disadvantages:
- Pupil can become dependant on this method
- Shallow water pools are not always available
- Not able to teach pupil to regain standing position
- Can cause over-confidence

Deep Water Method

The deep water method is a method by which pupils are encouraged to swim out of their depth. Encouraging pupils to swim out of their depth requires the teacher to have great care and understanding towards the pupils. They may have the ability but not the confidence or they may have become over-reliant on the shallow water method. Whatever the case, pupils may require some kind of buoyancy aid and you may require an assistant to be in the water with the pupils.

Advantages:
- Helps enhance strength and confidence in deep water
- May help encourage a regular breathing technique
- Promotes leg action

Disadvantages:
- Pupils can become over-confident
- Teaching larger groups can create greater risks
- Pupils' fear may hinder progress

Water Confidence

Much can be learned by pupils, especially children, by self-discovery. In other words, the teacher gives them a wide variety of ways to swim, move, jump, dive etc and the variety of what they are doing will give them new experiences. This in turn will cause them to learn almost by accident. The ability and confidence level of the pupils should be considered at all times, however. A pupil should want to do an activity and not be forced to do it. Forcing pupils can sometimes have the reverse effect on their confidence.

Entering the Water

For the non swimmer, entering the water can be hugely daunting or very exciting. Either way, it must be done in a safe and appropriate way. The following entries can be used accordingly:

Stepping in Using the Poolside Steps

This is the best entry for the nervous non-swimmer. They should be encouraged to hold on to the rails with both hands and step down one step at a time. This is a safe and gradual entry that allows the pupil to take their time. Therefore this method is very time consuming for larger groups.

The Sitting Swivel Entry

This entry is safest and quickest for larger groups. It also works best on deck-level swimming pools. From a sitting position, with legs in the water, the pupils should be instructed to place both hands to one side and then turn their backs to water. They should then lower themselves gradually into the water, keeping hold of the poolside at all times.

Jumping Entry

Before using a jumping entry, the teacher should consider the depth of the water compared to the size of the pupils. The pupils should then be instructed to start with their toes over the edge of the poolside, jump away from the poolside and bend their knees on landing. This entry is best for more confident pupils and should always be into water of a depth they are able to stand in.

Movement Through the Water

During the early stages of learning to swim, it is essential that pupils get used to the water slowly and gradually and, to a certain degree, at their own pace. Simple movements through the water such as walking or sliding their feet are very good confidence builders. Pupils should be encouraged to move around using their arms and hands whilst walking to get a 'feel' for the water.

Some pupils may require floats or buoyancy aids to support them whilst moving through the water. This will be more common in the nervous beginner and should be discouraged as soon as confidence begins to build, before pupils become dependant on them.

Movement patterns can take the form of shapes made on the pool floor with the feet, changes of direction, collecting a floating object such as a ball and, as confidence builds further, pupils can hop, skip and jump.

Underwater Confidence

The ability to submerge the face is arguably one of the most important stages of learning to swim. Some beginners arrive with this ability built in and only need to be taught how to breathe whilst swimming. For others it will be one of the most terrifying tasks they face. For these pupils it goes without saying, the 'softly softly' approach is needed! One stage at a time and only when the pupil is happy do you proceed to the next stage.

Stage 1: Getting the face wet

Remember: getting the face wet and being splashed in the face are two completely different concepts, each having different effects on pupils, and not always positive ones. Here are a few practices to work through:

- Blowing bubbles on the water surface or blowing an object along as they swim. Pupils can be encouraged to either blow gently 'like blowing through a straw' or blow with force 'like blowing out candles on a cake'.
- Cupping water in their own hands and throwing onto their face. This works well in a group as it can encourage one or two particularly anxious pupils to copy their peers. It should be done in a fun way but at the same time not forced on the nervous swimmer.
- Throwing and catching a ball is an excellent distraction from the splashes of the water. If the ball is made to land just in front of the pupil, this will result in a wet face without them realising. The smallest of splashes from the softest of throws will be sufficient to have a positive effect.

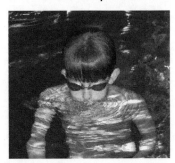  

Stage 2: Partially submerging the face

This is also best achieved with a gradual approach. Pupils first need to be taught how to hold their breath by 'breathing in and holding it all in'. Some will be able to do this easily, others will learn by trial and error as they partially submerge their face and realise they are not able to breath underwater! What ever the outcome, as a swimming teacher you must firstly treat these practices with caution and secondly enforce a fun learning environment to distract pupils from potential discomfort and distress.

An object can then be placed just under the water surface, shallow enough for the pupil to see and reach for it, but deep enough for the mouth to be submerged in order to reach it. Once confidence is gained with this exercise, then the object can be lowered slightly to encourage the mouth and nose to be submerged.

These practices are best performed with the teacher in the water holding the object him or herself. This may also help enhance pupils' confidence with the teacher in the water.

 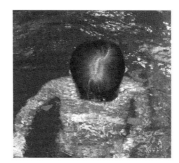

Stage 3: Total Submersion

Stage 2 naturally leads quickly onto stage 3 where the object is placed below the water surface and the pupil is encouraged to retrieve it by completely submerging their head underwater. By this stage, breath holding should be more accomplished and the pupil should begin to relax more as he or she submerges.

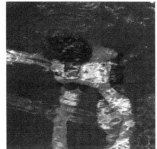

Progression from this stage is to incorporate face submerging, either partially or completely, whilst swimming various strokes and even retrieving objects from the pool floor during lengths or widths.

The Use of Goggles

There are varying opinions as to whether goggles should be used during swimming lessons or not. The advantages and disadvantages seem to balance out.

The first and most obvious advantage is that goggles enable pupils to see clearly under the water, therefore enhancing their confidence in putting their face into the water. This can be a particularly useful tool for teaching beginners or pupils with fear of getting their face wet, as the goggles can be portrayed as a new 'cool' thing to wear. After putting their face into the water, the sudden realisation that they can see clearly opens up a new world for them and confidence from then on is significantly boosted.

The main disadvantage is that some types of goggle can be uncomfortable to wear and pupils will constantly adjust, take off, put on and re-adjust their goggles, taking up valuable lesson time and distracting them away from the learning process. There is also the issue of them steaming up which, apart from impairing pupils' vision, also causes them to have to constantly clean them. This, once again, takes up valuable lesson and learning time. Nowadays 'anti fog' goggles can be purchased, as can 'anti fog' spray, to help prevent steaming up of goggles.

There is, of course, the issue of chemicals in the pool water and the sensitivity of children's eyes. Some children are more sensitive to pool water than others and in these circumstances it is advisable to wear goggles.

Fitting Goggles

Whilst wearing goggles is perfectly safe, putting them on and taking them off can be considered dangerous and requires pupils to be educated in this area. The elastic strap around the back of the head can cause the goggles to snap back if they are pulled away from the eyes and let go, resulting in injury to the eyes or face. Great care should be taken when fitting and removing goggles and educating pupils in this area is vital.

The safest way to fit goggles is to get the pupil to hold the eyes of the goggles onto their own eyes with one hand and then pull the elastic strap over their head with the other. The opposite then can be done when removing them, taking the strap over their head before removing the goggles from their eyes. Younger children and children who find this difficult should be encouraged to hold the goggles on their eyes with both hands whilst an adult fits or removes the elastic strap for them.

'Children require guidance and sympathy far more than instruction.'

Annie Sullivan

'A teacher is one who makes himself progressively unnecessary.'

Thomas Carruthers

Standing from a Prone Position

Aim: to regain a standing position from a prone position in the water. For complete beginners this can be started from holding the poolside or floats held under each arm. As confidence grows, the swimmer can attempt standing without assistance, which requires a greater use of the arms and hands. This can also be progressed to a moving exercise, moving first towards and then away from the poolside.

Teacher's Focus
- Movement should be relaxed and smooth
- Knees are drawn forward
- Arms pull downward and backwards
- Head should lift and face forward

Teaching Points
- Pull down and back with both arms
- Bend knees forwards as if to sit
- Lift head upwards
- Place feet on the pool floor

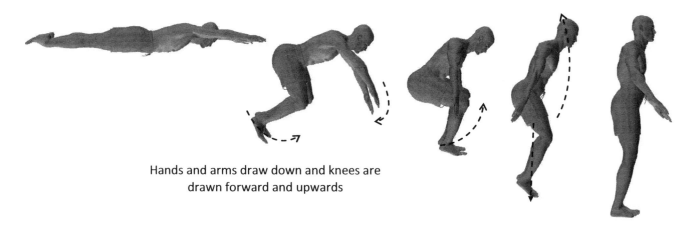

Hands and arms draw down and knees are drawn forward and upwards

Hands pull backwards as the head lifts and the feet are placed on the pool floor

Common Faults
- Rushed and not relaxed
- Failure to bend the knees
- Arching the back
- Failure to pull down and back

Standing from a Supine Position

Aim: to regain a standing position from a supine position in the water. For complete beginners this can be started from holding the floats or with a woggle held under the arms. As confidence grows the swimmer can attempt standing without assistance, which requires a greater use of the arms and hands. This can also be progressed to a moving exercise.

Teacher's Focus
- Movement should be relaxed and smooth
- Knees are drawn towards the chest
- Arms pull upwards and forwards
- Head should lift and face forward

Teaching Points
- Pull both arms upwards to the surface
- Bend knees forwards as if to sit
- Lift head upwards
- Place feet on the pool floor

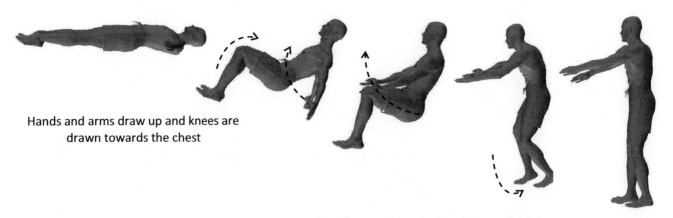

Hands and arms draw up and knees are drawn towards the chest

Hands pull upwards as the head lifts and the feet are placed on the pool floor

Common Faults
- Rushed and not relaxed
- Failure to bend the knees
- Arching the back
- Failure to pull up with both arms

The Strokes

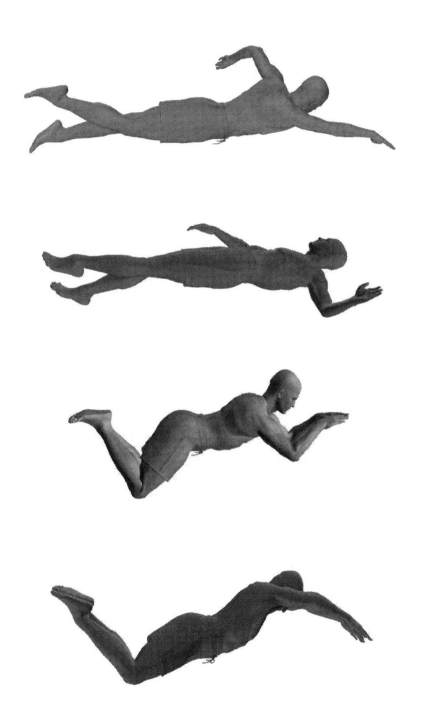

Front Crawl

Front crawl is the fastest, most efficient stroke of them all. This is largely down to the streamlined position of the body and continuous propulsion from the arms and legs. The alternating action of the arms and legs is relatively easy on the joints and the stroke as a whole develops aerobic capacity faster than any other stroke. In competitive terms it is usually referred to as Freestyle.

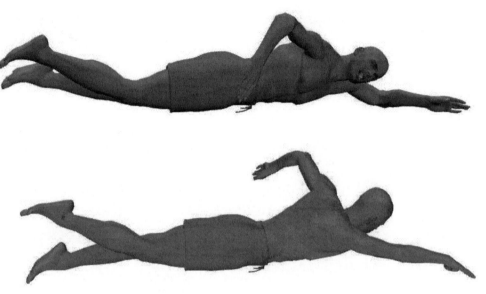

Body Position

- The overall body position is streamlined and as flat as possible at the water surface.
- The waterline is around the natural hairline with eyes looking forward and down.
- Shoulders remain at the surface and roll with the arm action.
- Hips also roll with the stroke close to the water surface.
- Legs remain in line with the body.

Leg Action

- The leg kick should originate from the hip and both legs should kick with equal force.
- Legs kick in an up and down alternating action, with the propulsive phase coming from the down kick.
- There should be a slight bend in the knee in order to produce the propulsion required on the down kick.
- Ankles are relaxed and toes pointed to give an in-toeing effect when kicking.
- Leg kick depth should be within the overall depth of the body.

Arm Action

Entry

- Continuous alternating action provides the majority of the power and propulsion of the entire stoke.
- Hand enters the water at a 45 degree angle, finger tips first, thumb side down. Hand entry should be between shoulder and head line with a slight elbow bend.

Catch

- The hand reaches forward under the water without over stretching.
- Arm fully extends just under the water surface.

Propulsive Phase

- Hand sweeps through the water downward, inwards and then upwards.
- Elbow is high at the end of the down sweep and remains high throughout the in-sweep.
- Hand pulls through towards the thigh and upwards to the water surface.

Recovery phase

- Elbow bends to exit the water first.
- Hand and fingers fully exit the water and follow a straight line along the body line over the water surface.
- Elbow is bent and high and the arm is fully relaxed.

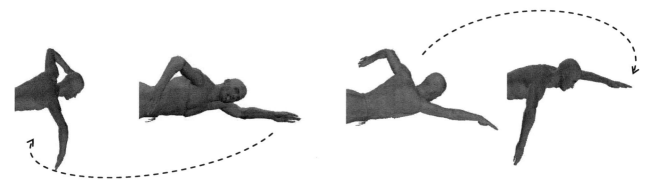

Breathing

- Head turns to the side on inhalation.
- Head begins to turn at the end of the upward sweep.
- Head turns enough for the mouth to clear the water and inhale.
- Head turns back into the water just as the arm comes over and hand returns to the water.
- Breathing can be bilateral or unilateral depending of the stroke cycle and distance to be swum.

Breathe IN

Breathe OUT

Timing

- Six beat cycle – each legs kicks three down kicks per arm cycle. The cycle is normally taught to beginners and used for sprint swims.
- Four beat cycle – each leg kicks down twice for each arm pull.
- Two-beat cycle – each leg kicks one downbeat per arm cycle. This timing cycle is normally used by long distance swimmers, where the leg kick acts as a counter balance instead of a source of propulsion. This is not recommended for beginners.
- Arms should provide a continuous power and propulsive alternating action whilst leg kicks also remain continuous and alternating.

Backstroke

Backstroke is the most efficient stroke swum on the back and is the third fastest of all swimming strokes. The majority of the power is produced by the alternating arm action and its horizontal streamlined position gives it its efficiency. Therefore Backstroke is the preferred stroke in competitive backstroke races.

Swimming on the back can be useful for helping a pupil to relax in the water. The nature of floating on the back, face up (supine) can be a calming and relaxing feeling. Also the face is clear of the water, allowing easy breathing and no water splashes onto the face. On the other hand it can be a counter productive at first, as it can give a feeling of disorientation and unease, as the pupil is facing upwards and therefore unaware of their surroundings. It is essential that pupils are taught how to regain a standing position from being supine in the water.

Body Position
- The supine body position is flat and horizontal, with ears slightly below the water surface.
- The head remains still throughout the stroke with the eyes looking slightly down the body at a point the swimmer is swimming away from.
- The hips and shoulder remains at or near the water surface but roll with the stroke.
- The legs remain together to maximise efficiency.

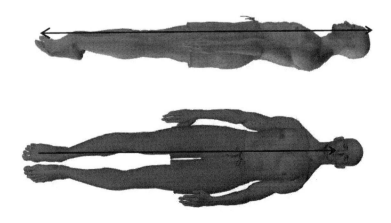

Leg Action
- The legs kick in an alternating action, continuously up and down to help balance the action of the arms.
- Legs should be stretched out with toes pointed (plantar flexed).
- Ankles should be relaxed and loose with toes pointing slightly inwards.
- The knee should bend slightly and then straighten as the leg kicks upwards.
- Toes should kick to create a small splash but not break the water surface.

Arm Action
Back crawl has two different arm actions that can be taught according to each pupil's ability and strength. The bent arm pull, which is the most efficient, and the straight arm pull, which is the easiest to learn. Therefore the straight arm pull is best for beginners.

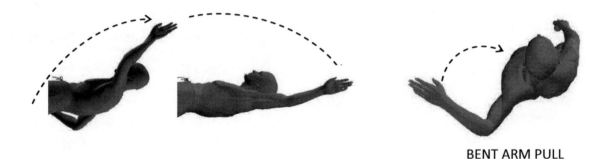

BENT ARM PULL

Straight Arm Pull
Entry
- The arm should be straight and as inline with the shoulder as possible. Hand should be turned with palm facing outwards and little finger entering the water first.

Propulsive phase
- The arm sweeps through the water in a semi-circle, pulling with force just under the water surface, pulling to the outside of the thigh.

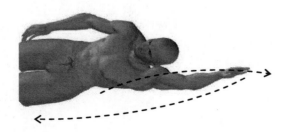

Bent Arm Pull

As the arm pulls through to completion, the overall path should follow an 'S' shape.

Entry

- The entry is the same as the straight arm pull, with the little finger entering first, the palm facing out and the arm close to the shoulder line.

Downward sweep

- The palm should always face the direction of travel.
- The shoulders roll and the elbow bends slightly as the arm sweeps downwards and outwards.

Upwards sweep

- As the hand sweeps inline with the shoulder, the palm changes pitch to sweep upwards and inwards.
- The elbow should then bend to 9o degrees and point to the pool floor.

Second Downward sweep

- The arm action then sweeps inwards towards the thigh and the palm faces downwards.
- The bent arm action is completed with the arm fully extended and the hand pushing downwards to counter balance the shoulder roll.

Recovery

- The thumb or the back of the hand should exit the water first.
- The shoulders roll again with the shoulder of the recovering arm rolling upwards.
- The arm rotates through 180 degrees over the shoulder.
- The palm is turned outwards during recovery to ensure that the hand enters the water little finger first.

Breathing

- Breathing should be in time with recovery of each arm, breathing in with one arm recovery and out with the other.
- A regular breathing pattern should be encouraged to prevent breath holding.

Timing

- Ideally there should be 6 leg kicks to one arm cycle. This may vary according to the swimmer's level of coordination.
- Arm action should be continuous. i.e. when one arm enters and begins to pull, the other should begin its recovery phase.

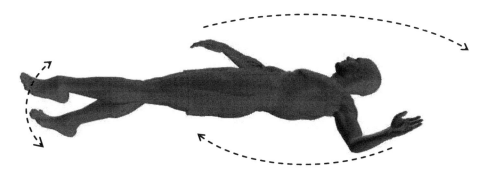

Breaststroke

Breaststroke is the oldest and slowest of the four swimming strokes.

It is also the most inefficient of all strokes, which is what makes it the slowest. Propulsion from the arms and legs is a consecutive action that takes place under the water. A large frontal resistance area is created as the heels draw up towards the seat and the breathing technique inclines the body, also increasing resistance. These are the main reasons that make breaststroke inefficient and slow.

Breaststroke is normally one of the first strokes to be taught, especially to adults, as the head and face is clear of the water, giving the swimmer a greater perception of their whereabouts and their buoyancy. There are variations in the overall technique for breaststroke, ranging from a slow recreational style to a more precise competitive style.

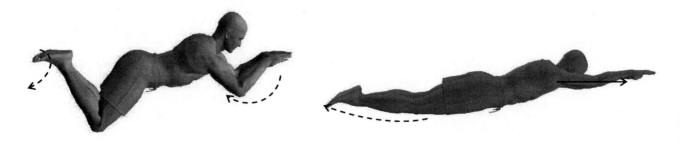

Body Position
- Body should be as flat and streamlined as possible with an inclination from the head to the feet so that the leg kick recovery takes place under the water.
- Head movement should be kept to a minimum and the shoulders should remain level throughout the stroke.
- As the propulsive phase of one part takes place, the opposite end of the body remains streamlined.

Leg Action

The most important teaching aspect of breaststroke legs is that the leg action is a series of movements that flow together to make one sweeping leg kicking action. It is important for a teacher to recognise the difference between the wedge kick and the whip kick. The leg action provides the largest amount of propulsion in the stroke and pupils will favour a wedge kick or a whip kick depending on which comes most naturally. The whip kick has a powerful whip action with the knees relatively close together and the wedge kick is a more pronounced and larger circular motion.

- The leg kick as a whole should be a simultaneous and flowing action, providing the majority of the propulsion.
- Knees bend as the heels are drawn up towards the seat.
- Toes are turned out ready for the heels and soles of the feet to drive the water backwards.
- Legs sweep outwards and downwards in a flowing circular path, accelerating as they kick.
- Legs return together and straight, providing a streamlined position.

  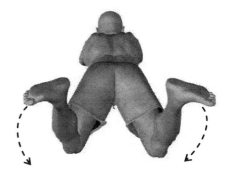

Arm Action

The amount of propulsion generated from the arm pull has developed over the years as the stroke has changed to become more competitive. The arm action overall provides the smallest propulsive phase of the four competitive strokes.

Catch
- Arm action begins with the arms fully extended out in front, fingers and hands together.
- Hands pitch outwards and downwards to an angle of about 45 degrees at the start of the catch phase.
- Arms pull outwards and downwards until they are approximately shoulder width apart.
- Elbows begin to bend and shoulders roll inwards at the end of the catch phase.

Propulsive phase
- Arms sweep downwards and inwards and the hands pull to their deepest point.
- Elbows bend to 90 degrees and remain high.
- At the end of the down sweep, the hands sweep inwards and slightly upwards.
- Elbows tuck into the sides as the hands are pulled inwards towards the chest and the chin.

Recovery
- Hands recover by stretching forwards in a streamlined position.
- Hands recover under, on or over the water surface, depending on the style of breaststroke to be taught.

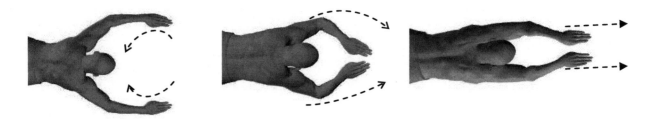

Breathing

Breaststroke action gives a natural body lift which gives the ideal breathing point with each stroke.
- Inhalation takes place at the end of the insweep as the body allows the head to lift clear of the water.
- Explosive or trickle breathing can be utilised.
- Head returns to the water to exhale as the arms stretch forward to begin their recovery phase.

Breathe IN   Breathe OUT

Timing

Breaststroke timing can be summed up in four words: pull, breath, kick, glide. A streamlined body position at the end of that sequence is essential to capitalise on the propulsive phases of the stroke. The timing can be considered in another way: when the arms are pulling in their propulsive phase, the legs are streamlined and when the legs are kicking in propulsion, the arms are streamlined. Full body extension is essential before the start of each stroke cycle.

Butterfly

Butterfly is the most recent stroke, developed in the 1953, and it is the second fastest stroke to Front Crawl. Butterfly evolved from Breaststroke as it also contains a simultaneous leg action and simultaneous arm action. The stroke requires a great deal of upper body strength and can be very physically demanding; therefore it is a stroke that is swum competitively rather than recreationally.

The undulating action of the body and the legs create great demands of the spine, therefore there are many alternative exercises and practices that can be used to make learning butterfly easier and less physical.

Body Position
The body position varies through the butterfly stroke cycle due to the continuous undulating action. The body should undulate from head to toe, producing a dolphin-type action.
- The body should be face down (prone) with the crown of the head leading the action.
- The shoulders should remain level throughout.
- The head should remain central and still, looking down until breathing is required.
- Hips should be inline with the shoulders and should remain parallel to the direction of travel

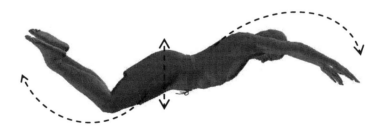

Leg Action
The main functions of the leg action are to balance the arm action and help to provide some propulsion. The legs kick simultaneously in an action that is similar to that of front crawl but with a greater and more pronounced knee bend.
- The upbeat of the kick should come from the hip.
- The ankles should be relaxed with toes pointed.
- Knees bend and then straighten on the downbeat to provide propulsion.
- Legs accelerate to provide power on the downbeat.

Arm Action

The arm action is a continuous simultaneous movement that requires significant upper body strength. The action of the arms is similar to that of front crawl and the underwater catch, down sweep and upsweep parts draw the shape of a 'keyhole' through its movement path.

Entry
- The entry of the hands into the water should be finger tips first, leading with the thumb.
- Fingers should be together with palms flat and facing outwards.
- Arms should be stretched forward with a slightly bent elbow.
- Entry should be with arms extended inline with the shoulders.

Catch and down sweep
- The pitch of the hands changes to a deeper angle with hands almost vertical.
- The catch and down sweep should begin just outside the shoulder line.
- Palms remain facing in the direction of travel.
- The elbow should bend to about 90 degrees to provide the extra power required.
- The hands sweep in a circular movement similar to breaststroke, but in a downwards path.

Upsweep
- The pitch of the hands changes to face out and upwards towards the water surface.
- Elbows extend fully to straighten the arms and hands towards the thighs.

Recovery
- Hands and arms must clear the water on recovery in accordance with ASA Law.
- Arms and hands should exit the water little finger facing upwards.
- Arms must clear the surface as they are 'thrown' over and forwards.
- Palms remain facing outwards, naturally giving a thumb-first entry.

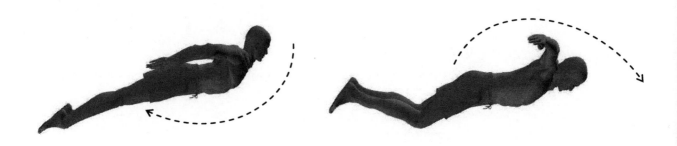

Breathing

- Inhalation takes place as the arms complete their upsweep and begin to recover, as the body begins to rise.
- The head is lifted and the chin should be pushed forward, but remain at the water surface.
- The head is lowered quickly into the water again as the arms recover inline with the shoulders.
- Explosive breathing is normally preferred but a combination of trickle and explosive breathing can be used.

Breathe IN

Breathe OUT

Timing

- The stroke cycle should contain 2 leg kicks to 1 arm cycle.
- The downbeat of the first leg kick occurs at the catch and down sweep phase.
- The second downbeat leg kick occurs during the upsweep phase of the arm cycle.
- Breathing can occur every stroke cycle or every other stroke cycle.

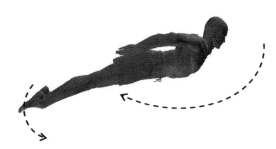

How to use this section

The page layout for each stroke practice follows the same format, keeping all relevant information for a given practice on one page. The aims and focuses, teaching points, common faults and corrective practices are all listed to make lesson planning easy and clear.

Below is an example page.

Stroke part
The aspect of the stroke being practiced

Description
A description and photograph of the stroke being practiced

Stroke
The stroke being practiced

Aim
The basic aim of the practice

Teachers Focus
Keys parts of the stroke practice to focus on

Teaching points
Key points to communicate

Diagram
A breakdown of the stroke practice

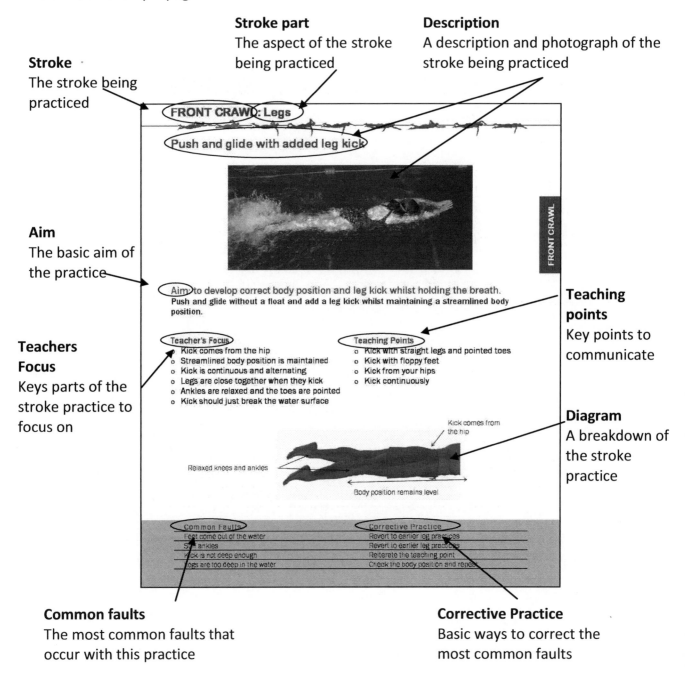

Common faults
The most common faults that occur with this practice

Corrective Practice
Basic ways to correct the most common faults

Stroke practices and teaching points can then be listed on lesson plans in accordance with the aims of the lesson.

The sample lesson plan below shows two stroke practices in the main theme section of the lesson

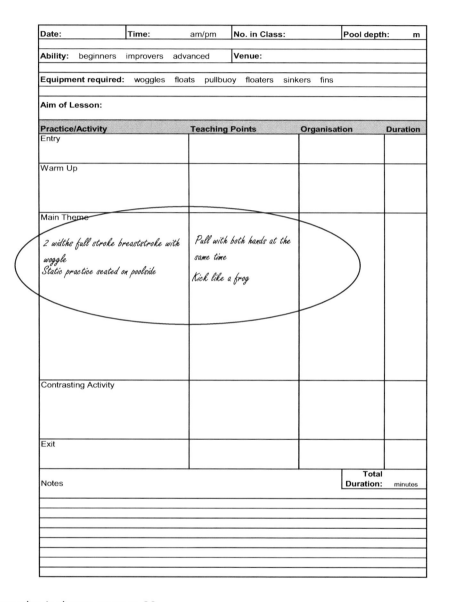

A completed lesson plan is shown on page 20.

<u>Stroke Practices</u>

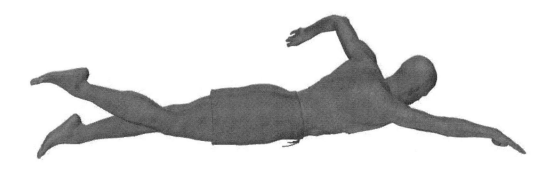

Front Crawl

FRONT CRAWL: Body Position

Holding the poolside

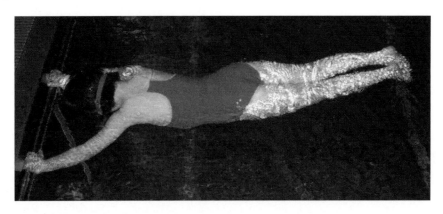

Aim: to encourage confidence in a floating position

The pupil holds the poolside for added security and some assistance may be required as some pupils will not naturally float.

Teacher's Focus
o Head is central and still
o Face is submerged
o Eyes are looking downwards
o Shoulders should be level
o Hips are close to the surface
o Legs are together and in line with the body

Teaching Points
o Relax
o Keep the head tucked between the arms
o Stretch out as far as you can
o Keep your feet together

Hands holding the poolside or rail

Overall body position is as horizontal as possible, depending on the swimmers own buoyancy.

Common Faults	Corrective Practice
Failure to submerge the face	Submerge the face from standing
Overall body is not relaxed	Reiterate the teaching point or assist
Head is not central	Reiterate the teaching point and repeat
Whole body is not remaining straight	Encourage relaxation
Feet are not together	Reiterate the teaching point and repeat

FRONT CRAWL: Body Position

Static practice holding floats

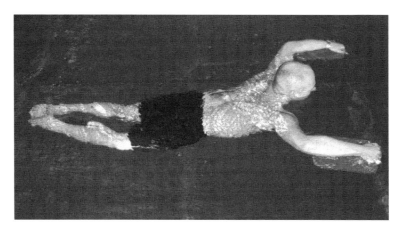

Aim: to help the swimmer develop confidence in his/her own buoyancy.

A float can be held under each arm or a single float held out in front, depending on levels of confidence and ability. Some swimmers may need extra assistance if they lack natural buoyancy.

Teacher's Focus
o Head is central and still
o Face is submerged
o Eyes are looking downwards
o Shoulders should be level
o Hips are close to the surface
o Legs are together and in line with the body

Teaching Points
o Relax
o Keep the head tucked between the arms
o Stretch out as far as you can
o Keep your feet together

Overall body position is horizontal and as flat as possible

Float held in each hand or single float held in both hands

Common Faults	Corrective Practice
Failure to submerge the face	Revert to the previous exercise
Head is not central	Reiterate the teaching point
Whole body is not remaining straight	Revert to the previous practice
Feet and hands are not together	Reiterate the teaching point

FRONT CRAWL: Body Position

Push and glide from standing

 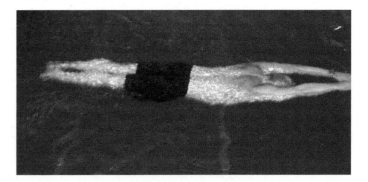

Aim: to develop correct body position and confidence in pushing off.

The swimmer can start with arms stretched out in front and pushes off from the pool floor or from the wall with one foot and glides through the water unaided.

Teacher's Focus
- o Initial push should be enough to gain good movement
- o Head remains still and central
- o Face submerged so that the water is at brow level
- o Shoulders should be level
- o Legs in line with the body

Teaching Points
- o Push hard from the side/pool floor
- o Keep your head tucked between your arms
- o Stretch out as far as you can
- o Keep your hands together
- o Keep your feet together

Direction of travel

Legs push off from pool side or pool floor

Common Faults	Corrective Practice
Failure to submerge the face	Revert to the previous practice
Push off is too weak	Reiterate the teaching point and practice
Whole body is not remaining straight	Reiterate the teaching point and practice
Feet are not together	Reiterate the teaching point and practice

FRONT CRAWL: Body Position

Push and glide from the side holding floats

Aim: to develop correct body position whilst moving through the water.

Body position should be laying prone with the head up at this stage. The use of floats helps to build confidence, particularly in the weak or nervous swimmer. The floats create a slight resistance to the glide, but this is still a useful exercise.

Teacher's Focus
o Head remains still and central with the chin on the water surface
o Eyes are looking forwards and downwards
o Shoulders should be level and square
o Hips are close to the surface
o Legs are in line with the body

Teaching Points
o Push hard from the wall
o Relax and float across the water
o Keep your head still and look forward
o Stretch out as far as you can
o Keep your feet together

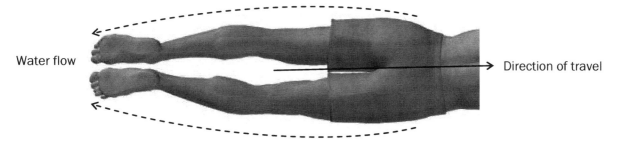

Water flow

Direction of travel

Streamlined body position minimises drag allowing efficient movement through the water

Common Faults	Corrective Practice
Push from the side is not hard enough	Reiterate the teaching point and repeat
Head is not central	Reiterate the teaching point and repeat
Whole body is not remaining straight	Revert to the previous practice
Feet are not together	Reiterate the teaching point and repeat

FRONT CRAWL: Body Position

Push and glide from the poolside

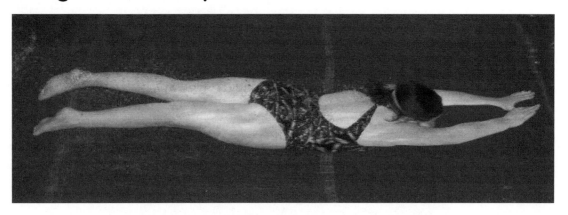

Aim: to develop a streamlined body position whilst moving thorough the water.

Movement is created by pushing and gliding from holding position at the poolside.

Teacher's Focus
o Head remains still and central
o Face submerged so that the water is at brow level
o Shoulders should be level and square
o Legs are in line with the body
o Overall body position should be streamlined

Teaching Points
o Push hard from the side
o Stretch your arms out in front as you push
o Keep your head tucked between your arms
o Stretch out as far as you can
o Keep your hands and feet together

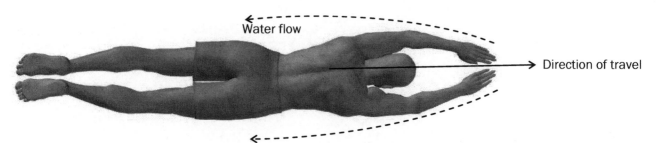

Streamlined body position minimises drag, allowing efficient movement through the water

Common Faults	Corrective Practice
Push off is too weak	Reiterate the teaching point and repeat
Arms stretch in front after the push	Standing practice with arms in front
Head is not central	Reiterate the teaching point and repeat
Overall body position not in line	Revert to the previous exercise
Hands or feet are not together	Reiterate the teaching point and repeat

FRONT CRAWL: Legs

Sitting on the poolside kicking

Aim: to give the swimmer the feel of the water during the kick.

Sitting on pool side kicking is an ideal exercise for the beginner to practise correct leg kicking action with the added confidence of sitting on the poolside.

Teacher's Focus
- o Kick is continuous and alternating
- o Knee is only slightly bent
- o Legs are close together when they kick
- o Ankles are relaxed and the toes are pointed.

Teaching Points
- o Kick with straight legs
- o Pointed toes
- o Make a small splash with your toes
- o Kick with floppy feet
- o Kick continuously

Kick comes from the hip →

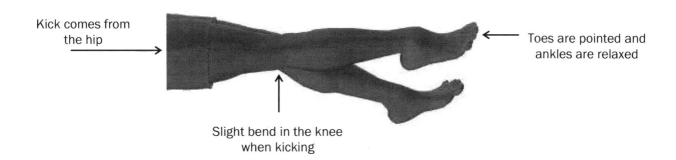

← Toes are pointed and ankles are relaxed

↑ Slight bend in the knee when kicking

Common Faults	Corrective Practice
Knees bend too much	Reiterate the teaching point and practice
Kick comes from the knee	Reiterate the teaching point and practice
Stiff ankles	Reiterate the teaching point

FRONT CRAWL: Legs

Holding the poolside

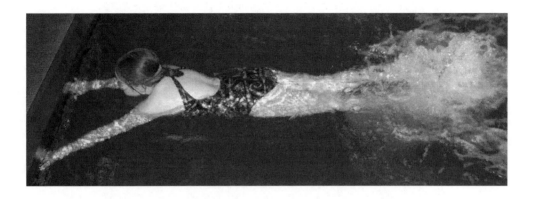

Aim: to encourage the swimmer to learn the kicking action.

Holding the poolside enhances confidence and helps develop leg strength.

Teacher's Focus
o Kick comes from the hip
o Kick is continuous and alternating
o Knee is only slightly bent
o Legs are close together when they kick
o Ankles are relaxed and the toes are pointed
o Kick should just break the water surface

Teaching Points
o Kick with straight legs
o Pointed toes
o Make a small splash with your toes
o Kick with floppy feet
o Kick from your hips
o Kick continuously
o Legs kick close together

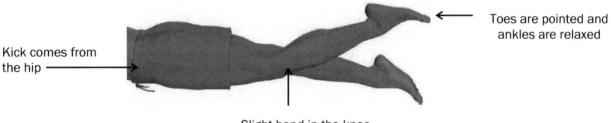

Kick comes from the hip

Toes are pointed and ankles are relaxed

Slight bend in the knee when kicking

Common Faults	Corrective Practice
Feet come out of the water	Check the body position and repeat
Kick comes from the knee	Reiterate the teaching point and repeat
Legs are too deep in the water	Check the body position and correct

FRONT CRAWL: Legs

Legs kick with a float held under each arm

Aim: to learn correct kicking technique and develop leg strength.
The added stability of two floats will help boost confidence in the weak swimmer.

Teacher's Focus
o Kick comes from the hip
o Kick is continuous and alternating
o Chin remains on the water surface
o Legs are close together when they kick
o Ankles are relaxed and the toes are pointed
o Kick should just break the water surface
o Upper body and arms should be relaxed

Teaching Points
o Kick with straight legs
o Pointed toes
o Kick with floppy feet
o Kick from your hips
o Kick continuously

Toes are pointed to provide streamline effect and ankles are relaxed

Downward kick provides propulsion

Common Faults	Corrective Practice
Head lifts above the surface, causing the legs to sink	Encourage face submersion
Kick comes from the knee causing excessive bend	Reiterate the teaching point or regress
Kick is not deep enough	Encourage kicking from the hips
Legs are too deep in the water	Check the body position and correct

FRONT CRAWL: Legs

Float held with both hands

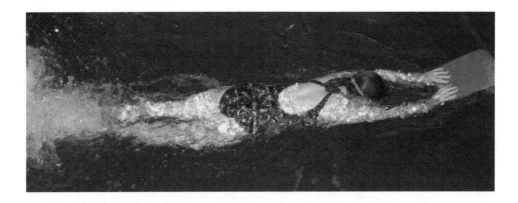

Aim: to practise and learn correct kicking technique.

Holding a float or kickboard out in front isolates the legs, encourages correct body position and develops leg strength.

Teacher's Focus
o Kick comes from the hip
o Kick is continuous and alternating.
o Legs are close together when they kick
o Ankles are relaxed and the toes are pointed.
o Kick should just break the water surface.

Teaching Points
o Kick with pointed toes
o Make a small splash with your toes
o Kick with floppy feet
o Legs kick close together

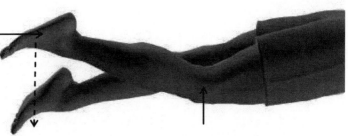

Toes are pointed to provide streamline effect and ankles are relaxed

Downward kick provides propulsion

Knee is relaxed and slightly bent

Common Faults	Corrective Practice
Knees bend too much	Revert to earlier leg practice
Feet come out of the water	Check the body position
Kick comes from the knee	Reiterate the teaching point
Legs are too deep in the water	Earlier body position practices

FRONT CRAWL: Legs

Push and glide with added leg kick

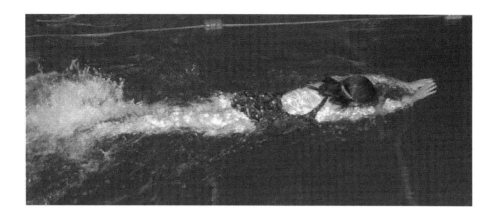

Aim: to develop correct body position and leg kick whilst holding the breath.

Push and glide without a float and add a leg kick whilst maintaining a streamlined body position.

Teacher's Focus
o Kick comes from the hip
o Streamlined body position is maintained
o Kick is continuous and alternating
o Legs are close together when they kick
o Ankles are relaxed and the toes are pointed
o Kick should just break the water surface

Teaching Points
o Kick with straight legs and pointed toes
o Kick with floppy feet
o Kick from your hips
o Kick continuously

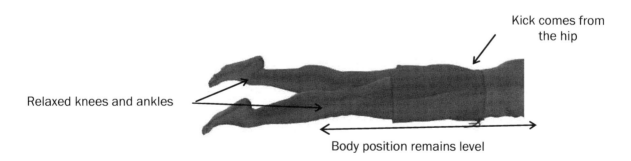

Kick comes from the hip

Relaxed knees and ankles

Body position remains level

Common Faults	Corrective Practice
Feet come out of the water	Revert to earlier leg practices
Stiff ankles	Revert to earlier leg practices
Kick is not deep enough	Reiterate the teaching point
Legs are too deep in the water	Check the body position and repeat

FRONT CRAWL: Legs

Leg kick whilst holding a float vertically in front

Aim: to create resistance and help develop strength and stamina.

Holding a float vertically in front increases the intensity of the kicking action which in turn develops leg strength and stamina.

Teacher's Focus
o Kick comes from the hip
o Streamlined body position is maintained
o Kick is continuous and alternating
o Legs are close together when they kick
o Ankles are relaxed and the toes are pointed
o Kick should just break the water surface

Teaching Points
o Kick with straight legs and pointed toes
o Kick with floppy feet
o Kick from your hips
o Kick continuously

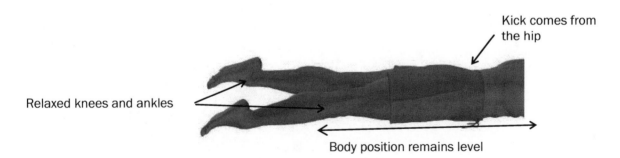

Kick comes from the hip

Relaxed knees and ankles

Body position remains level

Common Faults	Corrective Practice
Feet come out of the water	Regress to earlier leg practices
Stiff ankles	Regress to earlier leg practices
Kick is not deep enough	Reiterate the teaching point
Legs are too deep in the water	Check the body position and repeat

FRONT CRAWL: Arms

Standing on the poolside or in shallow water

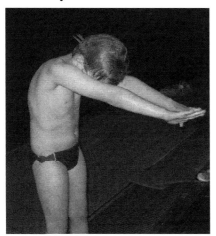 

Aim: to practise correct arm movement whilst in a static position.

This is an exercise for beginners that can be practised on the poolside or standing in shallow water.

Teacher's Focus
o Fingers should be together
o Pull through to the hips
o Elbow bends and leads upwards

Teaching Points
o Keep your fingers together
o Continuous smooth action
o Brush your hand past your thigh
o Gradually bend your elbow

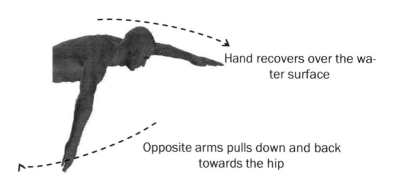

Elbow bends and leads upwards

Hand recovers over the water surface

Opposite arms pulls down and back towards the hip

Common Faults	Corrective Practice
Fingers are too wide apart	Reiterate the teaching point
Pull is short and not to the thigh	Encourage a longer pull
Arms are too straight as they pull	Encourage an elbow bend
Arms are too straight on recovery	Encourage an elbow bend
Hand entry is wide of the shoulder line	Reiterate through demonstration

FRONT CRAWL: Arms

Single arm practice with float held in one hand

Aim: to practise and improve correct arm technique

This practice allows the swimmer to develop arm technique whilst maintaining body position and leg kick. Holding a float with one hand gives the weaker swimmer security and allows the competent swimmer to focus on a single arm.

Teacher's Focus
o Fingertips enter first with thumb side down
o Fingers should be together
o Pull should be an elongated 'S' shape
o Pull through to the hips
o Elbow exits the water first
o Fingers clear the water on recovery

Teaching Points
o Keep your fingers together
o Brush your hand past your thigh
o Pull fast under the water
o Make an 'S' shape under the water
o Elbow out first
o Reach over the water surface

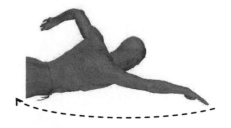

Elbow leads out of the water first

Arm pulls back through the water towards the hip

Common Faults	Corrective Practice
Fingers are apart	Reiterate the teaching point and repeat
Pull is short and not to the thigh	Revert to the previous arm exercise
Lack of power in the pull	Arms only to build strength
Arm pull is too deep underwater	Revert to the previous arm practice
Arms are too straight on recovery	Repeat the static standing practice

FRONT CRAWL: Arms

Alternating arm pull whilst holding a float out in front

Aim: to develop coordination and correct arm pull technique.

The swimmer uses an alternating arm action. This also introduces a timing aspect as the leg kick has to be continuous at the same time.

Teacher's Focus
o Clean entry with fingertips first and thumb side down
o Fingers should be together
o Each arm pulls through to the hips
o Elbow leads out first
o Fingers clear the water on recovery

Teaching Points
o Finger tips in first
o Brush your hand past your thigh
o Pull fast under the water
o Elbow out first
o Reach over the water surface

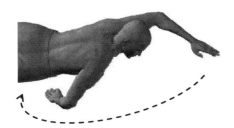

Arm pulls through towards the hip

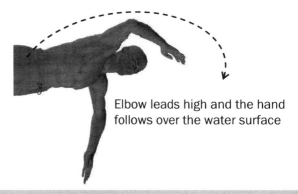

Elbow leads high and the hand follows over the water surface

Common Faults	Corrective Practice
Fingers are too wide apart	Reiterate the teaching point
Pull is short and not to the thigh	Repeat the previous arm exercise
Lack of power in the pull	Arms only to build up strength
Arms are too straight on recovery	Repeat the static standing practice
Hand entry is wide of shoulder line	Repeat the previous arm exercise

FRONT CRAWL: Arms

Arm action using a pull-buoy

Aim: to develop arm pull strength, technique and coordination.
This is a more advanced exercise which requires stamina and a degree of breathing technique.

Teacher's Focus
- o Fingertips enter first with thumb side down
- o Fingers should be together
- o Pull should be an elongated 'S' shape
- o Pull through to the hips
- o Elbow comes out first
- o Fingers clear the water on recovery

Teaching Points
- o Long strokes
- o Smooth continuous action
- o Brush your hand past your thigh
- o Make an 'S' shape under the water
- o Elbow out first
- o Reach over the water surface

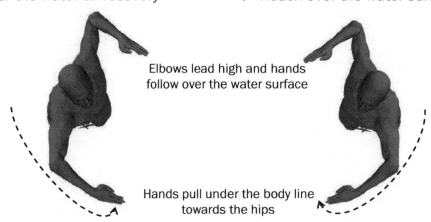

Elbows lead high and hands follow over the water surface

Hands pull under the body line towards the hips

Common Faults	Corrective Practice
Pull is short and not to the thigh	Revert to the earlier arm practice
Lack of power in the pull	Encourage power in the pull
Arms pull too deep under water	Revert to the earlier arm practice
Arms are too straight on recovery	Repeat the earlier standing practice
Hand entry is across the centre line	Reiterate and demonstrate

FRONT CRAWL: Arms

Push and glide adding arm cycles

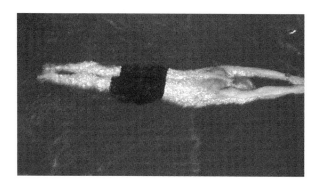 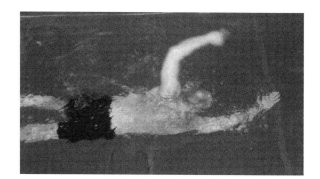

Aim: to combine correct arm action with a streamlined body position.

The swimmer performs a push and glide to establish body position and then adds arm cycles, whilst maintaining body position.

Teacher's Focus
- o Clean entry with fingertips first
- o Pull should be an elongated 'S' shape
- o Pull through to the hips
- o Elbow comes out first
- o Fingers clear the water on recovery

Teaching Points
- o Finger tips in the water first
- o Brush your hand past your thigh
- o Make an 'S' shape under the water
- o Elbow out first
- o Reach over the water surface

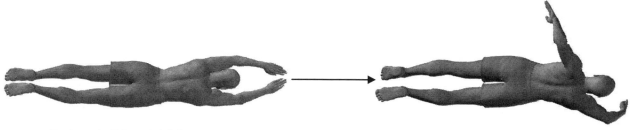

Push and glide establishes correct body position

Arm cycles are added

Common Faults	Corrective Practice
Pull is short and not to the thigh	Revert to the earlier arm practices
Lack of power in the pull	Earlier practices to build strength
Arms are too straight under water	Reiterate the teaching point and repeat
Arms are too straight on recovery	Reiterate the teaching point and repeat
Hand entry is across centre line	Revert to the previous arm practices

FRONT CRAWL: Breathing

Standing and holding the poolside

Aim: to practice and develop breathing technique.

The pupil stands and holds the pool rail with one arm extended, breathing to one side to introduce the beginner to breathing whilst having his/her face submerged.

Teacher's Focus
o Breathing should be from the mouth
o Breathing in should be when the head is turned to the side
o Breathing out should be when the face is down

Teaching Points
o Breathe out through your mouth
o Blow out slowly and gently
o Turn your head to the side when you breathe in
o See how long you can make the breath last

BREATHE IN

Head turns to the side and mouth clears the water surface

BREATHE OUT

Head faces forward and down

Common Faults	Corrective Practice
Breathing through the nose	Reiterate the teaching point
Holding the breath	Encourage breathing out

FRONT CRAWL: Breathing

Holding a float in front with diagonal grip

Aim: to encourage correct breathing technique whilst moving.

The float is held in front, one arm extended fully, the other holding the near corner with elbow low. This creates a gap for the head and mouth to be turned in at the point of breathing.

Teacher's Focus
o Breathing should be from the mouth
o Breathing in should be when the head is turned to the side
o Breathing out should be slow and controlled

Teaching Points
o Turn head towards the bent arm to breathe
o Breathe out through your mouth
o Blow out slowly and gently
o Return head to the centre soon after breathing

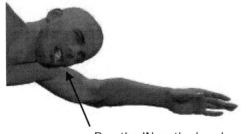

Breathe IN as the head turns out of the water

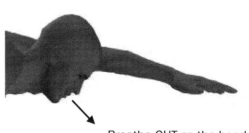

Breathe OUT as the head faces forward and down

Common Faults	Corrective Practice
Breathing through the nose	Revert to the earlier breathing practice
Holding the breath	Reiterate the teaching point
Lifting the head and looking forward when breathing	Reiterate the teaching point and repeat
Turning towards the straight arm	Reiterate the teaching point and repeat

FRONT CRAWL: Breathing

Float held in one hand, arm action with breathing

Aim: to develop correct breathing technique whilst pulling with one arm.

This allows the swimmer to add the arm action to the breathing technique and perfect the timing of the two movements. The float provides support and keeps the exercise as a simple single arm practice.

Teacher's Focus
o Head moves enough for mouth to clear the water
o Breathing in occurs when the head is turned to the side
o Breathing out should be slow
o Breathing should be from the mouth

Teaching Points
o Turn head to the side of the pulling arm
o Breathe out through your mouth
o Blow out slowly and gently
o Return head to the centre soon after breathing

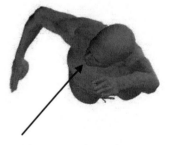

Breath IN as the arm pulls through and the head turns to the side

Common Faults	Corrective Practice
Turning towards the straight arm	Revert to the earlier breathing practice
Turning the head too much	Revert to the previous practice
Breathing through the nose	Reiterate the teaching point and repeat
Holding the breath	Reiterate the teaching point and repeat
Lifting the head and looking forward when breathing	Revert to earlier breathing practice

FRONT CRAWL: Breathing

Float held in both hands, alternate arm pull with breathing

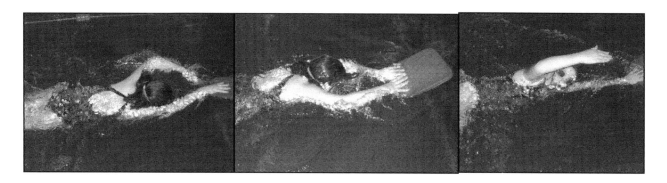

Aim: to practise bi-lateral breathing with the support of a float held out in front.

A single float is held in both hands and one arm pull is performed at a time with the head turning to breathe with each arm pull. Different arm action and breathing cycles can be used, for example; breathe every other arm pull or every three arm pulls.

Teacher's Focus

o Head should be still when not taking a breath
o Head movement should be minimal enough for mouth to clear the water
o Breathing in should be when the head is turned to the side
o Breathing should be from the mouth

Teaching Points

o Keep head still until you need to breathe
o Breathe every 3 strokes (or another pattern you may choose)
o Turn head to the side as your arm pulls back
o Return head to the centre soon after breathing
o Breathe out through your mouth

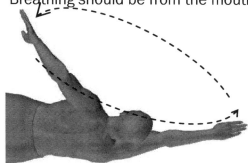

Head turns to the left side as the left arm pulls through and begins to recover

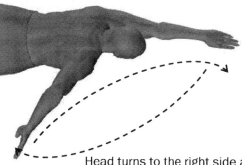

Head turns to the right side as the right arm pulls through and begins to recover

Common Faults	Corrective Practice
Turning towards the straight arm	Revert to the earlier practices
Turning the head too much	Revert to the previous practice
Turning the head too early or late to breath	Reiterate the teaching point and repeat
Lifting the head and looking forward when breathing	Revert to the earlier breathing practices

FRONT CRAWL: Timing

Front crawl catch up

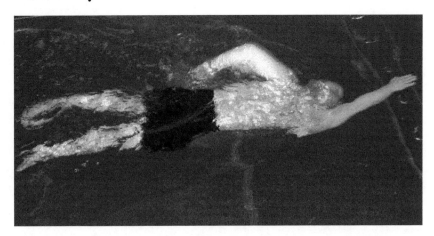

Aim: to practice correct stroke timing and develop coordination.

The opposite arm remains stationary until the arm performing the pull recovers to its starting position. This is an advanced exercise and encourages the swimmer to maintain body position and leg kick whilst practicing arm cycles.

Teacher's Focus
o   Clean entry with fingertips first
o   Pull should be an elongated 'S' shape
o   Pull through to the hips
o   Elbow comes out first
o   Fingers clear the water on recovery

Teaching Points
o   Finger tips in the water first
o   Brush your hand past your thigh
o   Make an 'S' shape under the water
o   Elbow out first
o   Reach over the water surface

Legs kick and hands are held together

One arm pulls and recovers as the opposite arm remains in front

Arm recovers to its position in front before the opposite arm pulls and recovers

Common Faults	Corrective Practice
One leg kick per arm pull ('one beat cycle')	Reiterate the teaching point and practice
Continuous leg kick but not enough arm pulls	Encourage rhythmic arm pull
Arm pull is too irregular	Encourage rhythmic arm pull

FRONT CRAWL: Full Stroke

Full stroke

Aim: to use full stroke Front Crawl demonstrating correct leg action, arm action, breathing and timing.

Teacher's Focus
o Stroke is smooth and continuous
o Head in line with the body
o Legs in line with the body
o Head remains still
o Leg kick is continuous and alternating
o Arm action is continuous and alternating
o Breathing is regular and to the side
o Stroke ideally has a 6 beat cycle

Teaching Points
o Keep your head still until you breathe
o Kick continuously from your hips
o Stretch forward with each arm action
o Pull continuously under your body
o Count 3 leg kicks with each arm pull

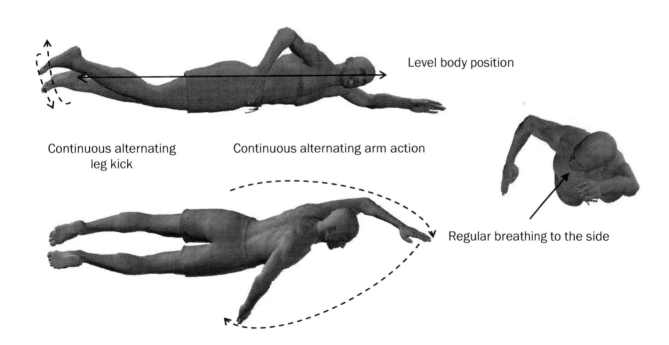

Level body position

Continuous alternating leg kick

Continuous alternating arm action

Regular breathing to the side

Common Faults	Corrective Practice
Head moves from side to side	Previous arm practices
Legs kick from the knee	Repeat earlier leg practices
Leg action is too slow	Repeat earlier leg practices
Arm action is untidy and splashing	Repeat earlier arm practices
Excessive head movement when breathing	Repeat previous breathing practices
Head is lifted, causing legs to sink	Repeat body position practices
Stroke is erratic and rushed	Check timing and repeat

Front Crawl

Exercise quick reference guide

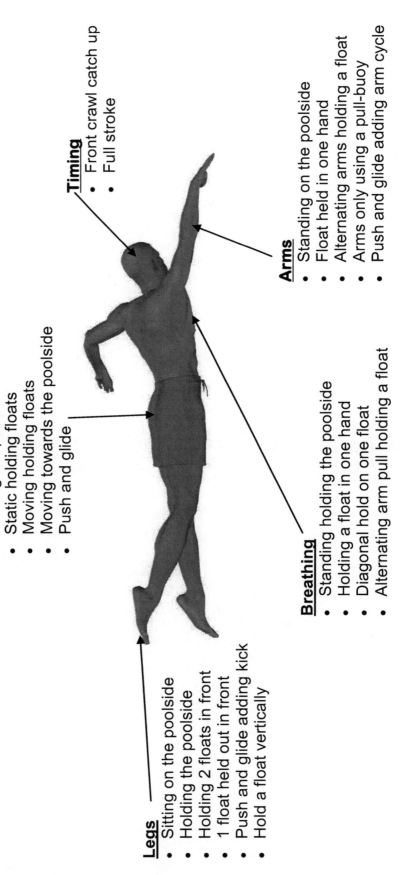

Body Position
- Holding the poolside
- Static holding floats
- Moving holding floats
- Moving towards the poolside
- Push and glide

Timing
- Front crawl catch up
- Full stroke

Arms
- Standing on the poolside
- Float held in one hand
- Alternating arms holding a float
- Arms only using a pull-buoy
- Push and glide adding arm cycle

Breathing
- Standing holding the poolside
- Holding a float in one hand
- Diagonal hold on one float
- Alternating arm pull holding a float

Legs
- Sitting on the poolside
- Holding the poolside
- Holding 2 floats in front
- 1 float held out in front
- Push and glide adding kick
- Hold a float vertically

<u>Stroke</u> Practices

Backstroke

BACKSTROKE: Body Position

Floating supine supported by floats

Aim: to gain confidence in a supine position on the water surface.

This exercise is ideal for the nervous swimmer. Support initially can be provided by the teacher, if he/she is also in the water. Support can then be provided by 2 floats, one placed under each arm, or by a woggle placed under both arms as in the photograph above.

Teacher's Focus
- o Overall body should be horizontal and streamlined
- o Head remains still
- o Eyes looking upwards and towards the feet
- o Hips must be close to the surface
- o Legs must be together

Teaching Points
- o Relax
- o Make your body flat on top of the water
- o Keep your head back
- o Push your tummy up to the surface
- o Look up to the ceiling
- o Keep your head still
- o Keep yourself in a long straight line

Body position remains level

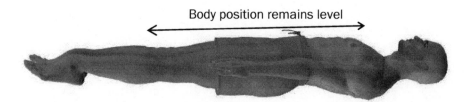

Common Faults	Corrective Practice
Head raises out of the water	Reiterate the teaching point
Tummy and hips sink	Reiterate the teaching point
Failing to maintain a flat position	Assist and encourage relaxation

BACKSTROKE: Body Position

Static supine position, holding a single float

Aim: to develop confidence in a supine position.

Holding a single float across the chest gives security to the nervous swimmer, but is not as stable as a woggle or a float under each arm and so is a subtle and gradual progression. If necessary, this exercise can be performed without a float, as shown in the diagram below, as an additional progression.

Teacher's Focus
- o Overall body should be horizontal
- o Head remains still
- o Eyes looking upwards
- o Hips must be close to the surface
- o Legs must be together

Teaching Points
- o Relax
- o Keep your head back
- o Push your tummy up to the surface
- o Look up to the ceiling
- o Keep your head still

Body position remains horizontal and relaxed

Common Faults	Corrective Practice
Head raises out of the water	Reiterate the teaching point and repeat
Eyes look up but head tips forward	Reiterate the teaching point and repeat
Tummy and hips sink	Revert to the previous practice
Head moves about	Reiterate the teaching point
Failing to maintain a straight line	Assist and encourage relaxation

BACKSTROKE: Body Position

Push and glide holding a float

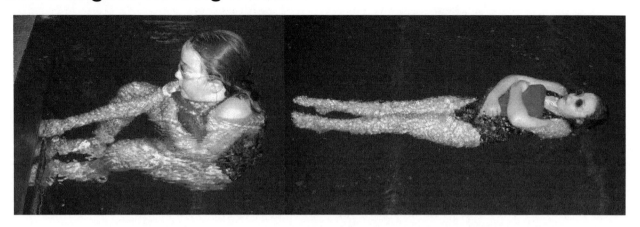

Aim: to gain confidence and move through the water in a supine position.

Holding a float gives added security to the nervous or weak swimmer whilst helping to maintain correct body position.

Teacher's Focus
- o Overall body should be horizontal and streamlined
- o Head remains still
- o Eyes looking upwards
- o Hips must be close to the surface
- o Legs must be together

Teaching Points
- o Relax
- o Keep your head back and chin up
- o Push your tummy up to the surface
- o Look up to the ceiling
- o Keep your head still
- o Push off like a rocket

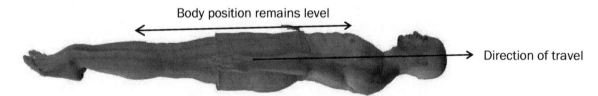

Body position remains level

Direction of travel

Float can be placed on the chest or behind the head as in the photos above.

Common Faults	Corrective Practice
Push off is not hard enough	Reiterate the teaching point and repeat
Head raises out of the water	Repeat the previous body position practice
Tummy and hips sink	Reiterate the teaching point and repeat
Failing to maintain a straight line	Assist and encourage relaxation

BACKSTROKE: Body Position

Push and glide from the poolside without floats

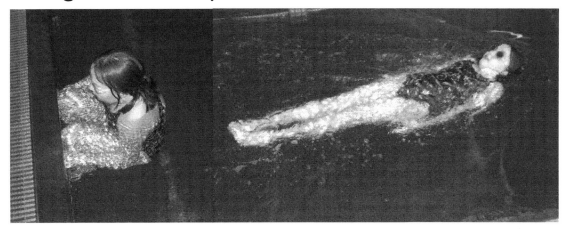

Aim: to encourage correct body position whilst moving.

The swimmer uses the momentum of a push from the pool side. Arms are held by the sides or held straight over the head in more advanced cases.

Teacher's Focus
o Overall body should be horizontal and streamlined
o Head remains still
o Eyes looking upwards and towards the feet
o Hips must be close to the surface
o Legs must be together
o Arms are held by the sides

Teaching Points
o Relax
o Make your body as long as you can
o Push off like a rocket
o Push your tummy up to the surface
o Look up to the ceiling
o Glide in a long straight line

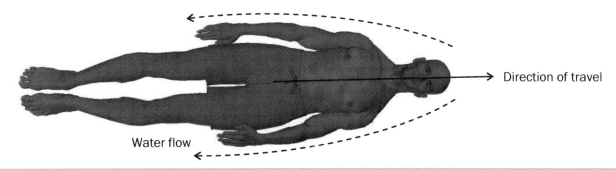

Direction of travel

Water flow

Common Faults	Corrective Practice
Push off is not hard enough	Reiterate the teaching point and repeat
Head raises out of the water	Reiterate the teaching point and repeat
Tummy and hips sink	Repeat the previous practice with float
Failing to maintain a straight line	Reiterate the teaching points and repeat

BACKSTROKE: Legs

Static practice, sitting on the poolside

Aim: to develop an alternating leg kick action.

The swimmers is positioned sitting on the pool side with feet in the water. Ideal for the nervous beginner to get accustomed to the 'feel' of the water.

Teacher's Focus
o Kick comes from the hips
o Toes are pointed
o Legs are together
o Slight knee bend
o Ankles are relaxed

Teaching Points
o Point your toes like a ballerina
o Kick from your hips
o Kick with floppy feet
o Keep your legs together
o Make your legs as long as possible

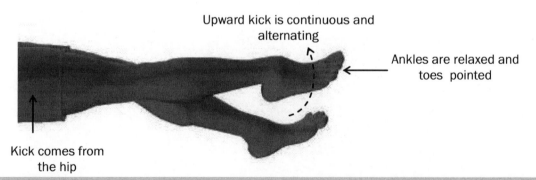

Upward kick is continuous and alternating

Ankles are relaxed and toes pointed

Kick comes from the hip

Common Faults	Corrective Practice
Kick comes from the knee	Reiterate teaching point and repeat
Legs kick apart	Check body position and repeat
Toes are turned up	Reiterate teaching point and repeat
Legs are too 'stiff', not relaxed	Encourage to relax and repeat

BACKSTROKE: Legs

Woggle held under the arms

Aim: to practise and develop correct leg kick action.

This exercise is ideal for the nervous beginner as an introduction to swimming on the back. The stability of the woggle encourages kicking and motion backwards with ease.

Teacher's Focus
- o Kick comes from the hips
- o Kick is alternating and continuous
- o Kick breaks the water surface
- o Hips and tummy up near the surface
- o Toes are pointed and ankles relaxed
- o Legs are together
- o Slight knee bend

Teaching Points
- o Point your toes like a ballerina
- o Kick from your hips
- o Kick with floppy feet
- o Make a small splash with your toes

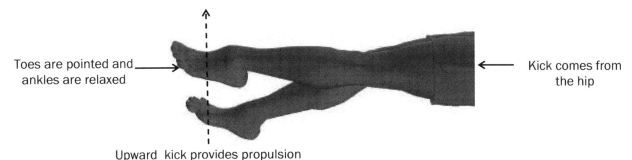

Toes are pointed and ankles are relaxed

Kick comes from the hip

Upward kick provides propulsion

Common Faults	Corrective Practice
Kick comes from the knee	Reiterate teaching point and repeat
Hips sink and legs kick too deep	Check body position and repeat
Toes are turned up	Reiterate teaching point and repeat
Stiff ankles	Repeat previous leg practice
Legs are too 'stiff', not relaxed	Encourage the pupil to relax and repeat

BACKSTROKE: Legs

Float held under each arm

Aim: to practise and develop leg action whilst maintaining correct body position.
Two floats provide good support and encourage a relaxed body position, without creating excessive resistance through the water.

Teacher's Focus
o Kick breaks the water surface
o Hips and tummy are up near the surface
o Toes are pointed and ankles relaxed
o Legs are together
o Slight knee bend
o Ankles are relaxed

Teaching Points
o Relax and kick hard
o Point your toes like a ballerina
o Kick from your hips
o Kick with floppy feet
o Make a small splash with your toes
o Keep your legs together

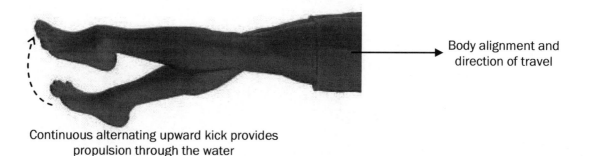

Body alignment and direction of travel

Continuous alternating upward kick provides propulsion through the water

Common Faults	Corrective Practice
Toes are turned up, causing a lack of motion	Reiterate the teaching point and repeat
Head comes up, causing legs to sink	Repeat the earlier body position practices
Hips sink and legs kick too deep	Check the body position and repeat
Legs kick apart	Reiterate the teaching point and repeat

BACKSTROKE: Legs

Float held on the chest

Aim: to allow the correct body position to be maintained whilst the legs kick.

This is a progression from having a float held under each arm. The swimmer is less stable but still has the security of one float held on the chest.

Teacher's Focus
- o Kick comes from the hips
- o Kick is alternating and continuous
- o Kick breaks the water surface
- o Hips and tummy up near the surface
- o Legs are together
- o Ankles are relaxed and toes pointed

Teaching Points
- o Point your toes like a ballerina
- o Kick from your hips
- o Kick with floppy feet
- o Make a small splash with your toes
- o Keep your legs together

Ankles are relaxed and toes pointed to provide power to the upward kick

Body position remains level

Kick comes from the hip

Common Faults	Corrective Practice
Kick comes from the knee	Reiterate the teaching point and repeat
Legs are too deep	Repeat the previous leg practice
Toes are turned up	Repeat the earlier poolside practice
Stiff ankles	Reiterate the teaching point
Legs are too 'stiff', not relaxed	Encourage the pupil to relax and repeat

BACKSTROKE: Legs

Float held behind the head

Aim: to encourage correct body position as the legs kick.

The float behind the head helps to keep the chest and hips high. A variation of the exercise with the float held on the chest, this exercise helps to develop leg strength and stamina.

Teacher's Focus
o Kick comes from the hips
o Kick breaks the water surface
o Hips and tummy up near the surface
o Toes are pointed and ankles relaxed
o Legs are together

Teaching Points
o Kick from your hips
o Kick with floppy feet
o Make a small splash with your toes
o Keep your legs together

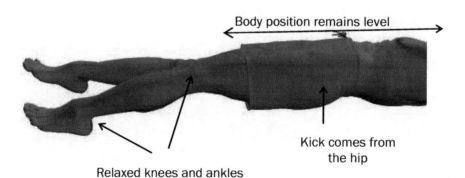

Body position remains level

Kick comes from the hip

Relaxed knees and ankles

Common Faults	Corrective Practice
Kick comes from the knee	Repeat the earlier leg practices
Legs are too deep	Check the body position and repeat
Toes are turned up	Reiterate the teaching point and repeat
Stiff ankles	Reiterate the teaching point and repeat
Legs too 'stiff', not relaxed	Encourage the pupil to relax and repeat

BACKSTROKE: Legs

Float held over the knees

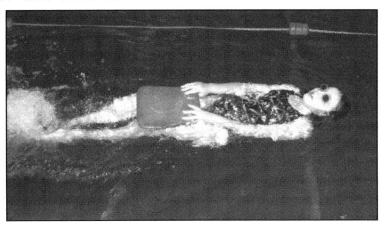

Aim: to prevent excessive knee bend by holding a float over the knees.

This kicking practice should be performed with the float held on the water surface without the knees hitting it as they kick.

Teacher's Focus
o Kick comes from the hips
o Legs kick without touching the float
o Kick breaks the water surface
o Hips and tummy up near the surface
o Toes are pointed and ankles relaxed

Teaching Points
o Kick with straight legs
o Point your toes like a ballerina
o Stop your knees hitting the float
o Kick with floppy feet

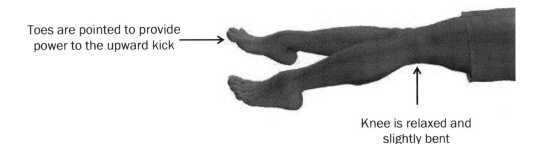

Toes are pointed to provide power to the upward kick →

Knee is relaxed and slightly bent

Common Faults	Corrective Practice
Kick comes from the knee	Reiterate the teaching point and repeat
Knees bend and hit the float	Encourage a kick from the hip
Leg kick is too deep	Check the body position and repeat
Float is held up above the water surface	Demonstrate and repeat

BACKSTROKE: Legs

Float held overhead with arms straight

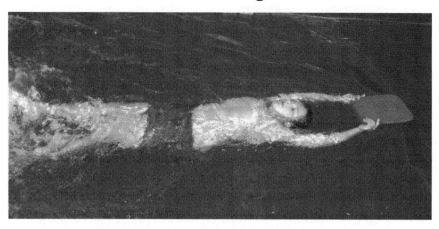

Aim: to enhance a correct body position whilst kicking.

This exercise is a progression from previous leg kick exercises and helps to develop a stronger leg kick.

Teacher's Focus
o Kick comes from the hips
o Arms remain either side of the head
o Kick breaks the water surface
o Hips and tummy up near the surface

Teaching Points
o Push your hips and chest up to the surface
o Point your toes like a ballerina
o Make your whole body long and straight
o Kick from your hips
o Stretch out and kick hard

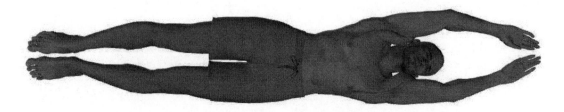

Legs kick and correct body position is maintained throughout.
Note: advanced alternative is shown without holding a float.

Common Faults	Corrective Practice
Head is raised causing hips and legs to sink	Check the body position and repeat
Hips sink and legs kick too deep	Repeat the earlier body position practices
Toes are turned up	Reiterate the teaching point and repeat
Head is too far back and the upper body sinks	Repeat earlier body position practices

BACKSTROKE: Legs

Kicking with arms by the sides, hands sculling

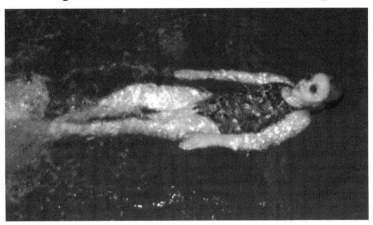

Aim: to practise kicking and maintaining correct body position on the back.

The sculling hand action provides balance and enhances confidence.

Teacher's Focus
- o Kick comes from the hips
- o Kick is alternating and continuous
- o Kick breaks the water surface
- o Hips and tummy up near the surface
- o Ankles are relaxed and toes are pointed

Teaching Points
- o Relax
- o Push your hips and chest up to the surface
- o Point your toes like a ballerina
- o Kick with floppy feet
- o Look up to the sky

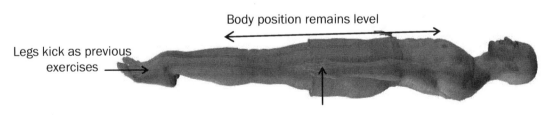

Body position remains level

Legs kick as previous exercises

Hands sculling by the sides

Common Faults	Corrective Practice
Kick comes from the knee	Repeat the earlier leg practices
Hips sink and legs kick too deep	Repeat the body position practices
Head is too far back	Repeat the earlier body position practices
Body is not relaxed	Repeat the earlier practices with floats

BACKSTROKE: Arms

Static practice standing on the poolside

Aim: to practise the arm action in its most basic form.

Standing on the poolside allows the swimmer to develop basic technique in a static position.

Teacher's Focus
o Arm action is continuous
o Arms stretch all the way up and brush past the ear
o Arms pull down to the side, towards the hip

Teaching Points
o Arms brush past your ear
o Fingers closed together
o Arms are continuous
o Stretch your arm all the way up to your ear
o Pull down to your side

Arm rises upwards, little finger leading and arm brushing the ear

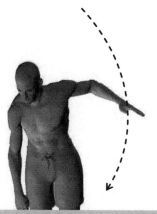

Hand pulls downwards toward the hip

Common Faults	Corrective Practice
Arms are not raising to touch the ear	Demonstrate and repeat
Arms are not pulling down to the side	Demonstrate and repeat
Pausing in-between arm pulls	Reiterate the teaching point and repeat
Arms are bending over the head	Demonstrate and repeat

BACKSTROKE: Arms

Single arm pull with a float held on the chest

Aim: to develop correct arm action whilst kicking.

The float held on the chest provides support for the beginner and the single arm action allows easy learning without compromising the swimmer's coordination.

Teacher's Focus
- o Arm action is continuous
- o Arms stretch all the way up and brush past the ear
- o Arms pull down to the thigh
- o Fingers are together
- o Little finger enters water first

Teaching Points
- o Arm brushes past your ear
- o Pull down to your thigh
- o Fingers closed together
- o Little finger enters the water first

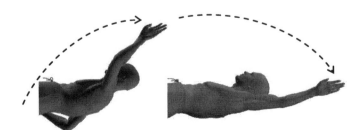

Arm exits the water and brushes past the ear, entering the water little finger first

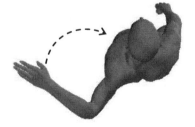

Arm is bent as it pulls through and straightens as it pulls to the thigh

Common Faults	Corrective Practice
Arms are pulling out too wide, not brushing the ear	Reiterate the teaching point and repeat
Arms are not pulling down to the side	Reiterate the teaching point and repeat
Arms pull too deep under the water	Repeat the previous arm practice
Fingers are apart	Reiterate teaching point and repeat
Thumb enters the water first	Repeat previous arm practice

BACKSTROKE: Arms

Single arm pull using the lane rope

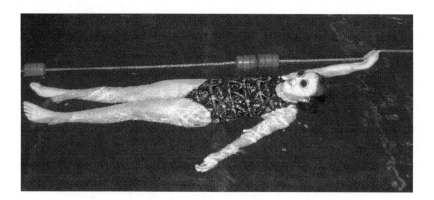

Aim: to develop a bent arm pull using the lane rope to move though the water.

The hand remains fixed on the lane rope as the body is pulled along in the line of the rope. This simulates the bent arm pull action.

Teacher's Focus
o Arm action is continuous
o Arms stretch all the way up and brush past the ear
o Arms pull down to the thigh
o Arm action is continuous
o Thumb comes out first

Teaching Points
o Use the rope to pull you along
o Arms brush past your ear
o Stretch over and hold the rope behind
o Pull fast down the rope
o Thumb comes out first
o Little finger enters the water first

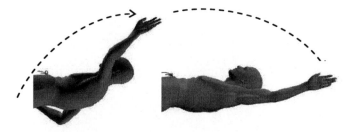

Arm exits the water and brushes past the ear, entering the water little finger first, taking hold of the lane rope

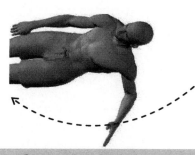

Swimmer pulls from above the head and then pushes past the hip to simulate the bent arm pull action

Common Faults	Corrective Practice
Arms are not pulling down to the side	Demonstrate and repeat
Elbow is not bending enough	Reiterate the teaching point and repeat
Arms are bending over the head	Repeat the earlier arm practices
Thumb enters the water first	Repeat the earlier arm practices

BACKSTROKE: Arms

Single arm pull with the opposite arm held by the side

Aim: to practise correct arm action without the aid of floats.

This single arm exercise allows focus on one arm whilst the arm held by the side encourages correct body position.

Teacher's Focus
- Arm action is continuous
- Arms stretch all the way up and brush past the ear
- Arms pull down to the thigh
- Shoulders rock with each arm pull
- Little finger enters the water first

Teaching Points
- Arms brush past your ear
- Arms are continuous
- Pull down to your side
- Pull fast through the water
- Little finger enters the water first

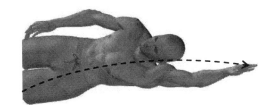

Arm rises upwards, little finger leading and arm brushing the ear

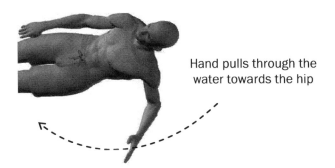

Hand pulls through the water towards the hip

Common Faults	Corrective Practice
Arms are pulling out too wide, not brushing the ear	Repeat the earlier arm practices
Arms are not pulling down to the side	Reiterate the teaching point and repeat
Arms pull too deep under the water	Repeat the previous arm practice
Arms are bending over the head	Repeat the earlier arm practices

BACKSTROKE: Arms

Arms only with pull-buoy held between legs

Aim: to develop a continual arm action using both arms.

The pull-buoy provides support and helps to isolate the arms by preventing the leg kick action. Note: it is normal for the legs to 'sway' from side to side.

Teacher's Focus
- o Arm action is continuous and steady
- o Arms stretch all the way over and brush past the ear
- o Arms pull down to the thigh
- o Shoulders rock evenly side to side

Teaching Points
- o Arms brush past your ear
- o Fingers closed together
- o Continuous arm action
- o Pull hard through the water and down to your side
- o Allow your legs to 'sway' side to side

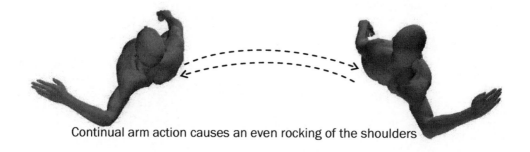

Continual arm action causes an even rocking of the shoulders

Common Faults	Corrective Practice
Pause between arm pulls	Repeat the poolside standing practice
Arms are pulling out too wide, not brushing the ear	Reiterate the teaching point and repeat
Arms are not pulling down to the side	Repeat the previous arm practice
Arms pull too deep under the water	Repeat the previous arm practice

BACKSTROKE: Breathing

Full stroke with breathing

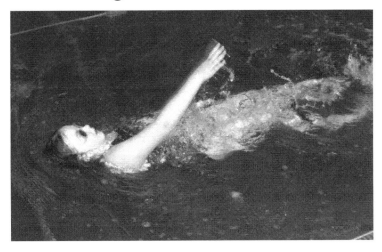

Aim: to focus on breathing in time with the stroke actions.

The swimmer should breathe in and out in regular rhythm with the arm action. This exercise can be incorporated into any of the previous arm action exercises, depending on the ability of the swimmer.

Teacher's Focus
o Breathing should be regular and rhythmical

Teaching Points
o Breathe in time with your arms
o Breathe in with one arm pull and out with the other

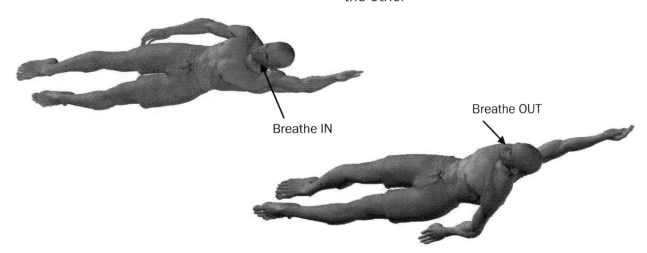

Breathe IN

Breathe OUT

Common Faults	Corrective Practice
Holding the breath	Repeat the static breathing practices
Breathing too rapidly	Reiterate the teaching point and repeat

BACKSTROKE: Timing

Push and glide adding arms and legs

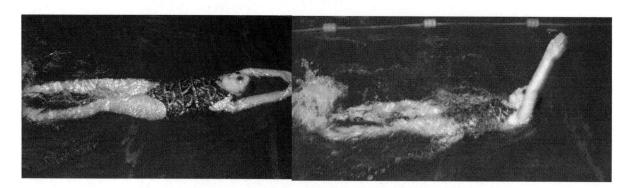

Aim: to practise and develop coordination and stroke timing.

The swimmer performs a push and glide to establish correct body position, then adds arm and leg actions.

Teacher's Focus

o   3 leg kicks per arm pull
o   Leg kick should be continuous
o   Arm action should be regular

Teaching Points

o   Count in your head to 3 with each arm pull
o   Kick 3 times with each arm pull
o   Keep the arm pull continuous
o   Keep the leg kick continuous

One arm exits the water as the other begins to pull and
the leg kick remains continuous

Common Faults	Corrective Practice
One leg kick per arm pull ('one beat cycle')	Reiterate the teaching point and repeat
Continuous leg kick but not enough arm pulls	Repeat the earlier arm practices
Arm pull is too irregular	Repeat the earlier arm practices
Stroke cycle is not regular and continuous	Reiterate the teaching point and repeat

BACKSTROKE: Full Stroke

Full stroke

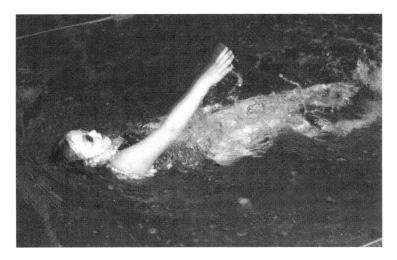

Aim: to demonstrate full stroke backstroke showing continuous and alternating arm and leg actions, with correct timing, resulting in a smooth and efficient stroke.

Teacher's Focus
o Body position should be horizontal and flat
o Leg kick should be continuous and alternating
o Arm action is continuous
o Leg kick breaks the water surface
o 3 legs kicks per arm pull

Teaching Points
o Kick from your hips
o Relax
o Keep your hips and tummy at the surface
o Make a small splash with your toes
o Continuous arm action
o Arms brush past your ear and pull to your side

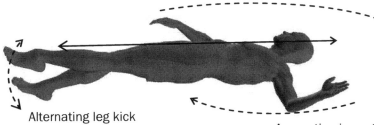

Body position remains level

Alternating leg kick remains at the water surface

Arm action is continuous and alternating

Common Faults	Corrective Practice
Hips and abdomen sink	Repeat the earlier body position practice
Legs kick too deep or weak	Repeat the earlier leg practices
Arms pull one at a time	Repeat the earlier arm practices
Arms pull too wide or too deep	Reiterate the teaching point and repeat

Backstroke

Exercise quick reference guide

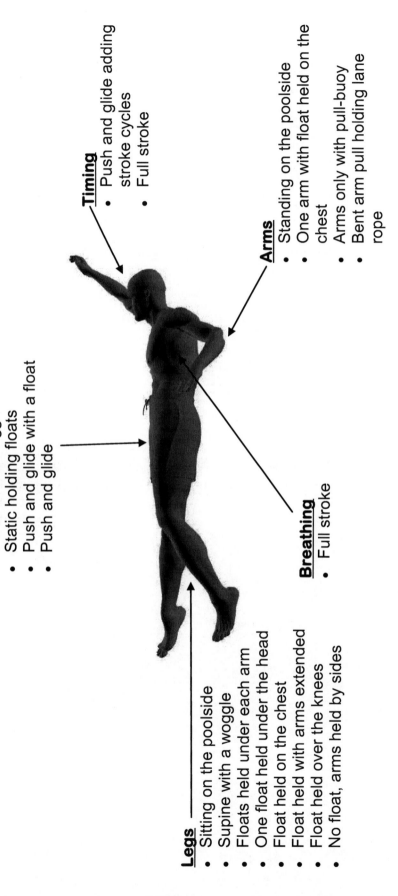

Body Position
- Static with a woggle
- Static holding floats
- Push and glide with a float
- Push and glide

Legs
- Sitting on the poolside
- Supine with a woggle
- Floats held under each arm
- One float held under the head
- Float held on the chest
- Float held with arms extended
- Float held over the knees
- No float, arms held by sides

Timing
- Push and glide adding stroke cycles
- Full stroke

Arms
- Standing on the poolside
- One arm with float held on the chest
- Arms only with pull-buoy
- Bent arm pull holding lane rope

Breathing
- Full stroke

96

Stroke Practices

Breaststroke

BREASTSTROKE: Body Position

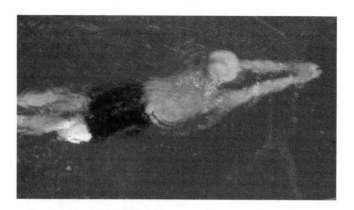

Push and glide

Aim: to develop a basic body position by pushing from the side

The distance of the glide will be limited due to the resistance created by the chest and shoulders. The exercise can be performed with the face submerged as it would be during the glide phase of the stroke or with the head up facing forwards.

Teacher's Focus
o Head remains still and central
o Face is up so that only the chin is in the water
o Eyes are looking forwards over the surface
o Shoulders should be level and square
o Hips are slightly below shoulder level
o Legs are in line with the body

Teaching Points
o Push hard from the side
o Keep head up looking forward
o Stretch out as far as you can
o Keep your hands together
o Keep your feet together

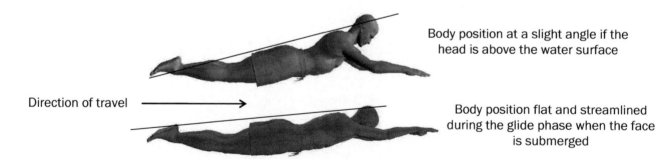

Body position at a slight angle if the head is above the water surface

Direction of travel

Body position flat and streamlined during the glide phase when the face is submerged

Common Faults	Corrective Practice
Shoulders and/or hips are not level	Reiterate the teaching point and repeat
Head is not central and still	Reiterate the teaching point and repeat
One shoulder is in front of the other	Encourage a straight line glide

BREASTSTROKE: Legs

Sitting on the poolside with feet in the water

Aim: to practice the leg action whilst sat stationary on the poolside.

This exercise allows the pupil to copy the teacher who can also be sat on the poolside demonstrating the leg kick. The physical movement can be learnt before attempting the leg kick in the water.

Teacher's Focus
o Kick should be simultaneous
o Legs should be a mirror image
o Heels are drawn towards the seat
o The feet turn out just before the kick
o Feet come together at the end of the kick with legs straight and toes pointed

Teaching Points
o Kick your legs simultaneously
o Keep your knees close together
o Kick like a frog
o Make sure your legs are straight and together at the end of the kick

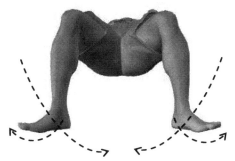

Feet turn out as the legs begin to kick round in a circular action

Common Faults	Corrective Practice
Circular kick in the opposite direction	Demonstrate and repeat
Only turning one foot out	Demonstrate and repeat
Legs are not straight at the end of the kick	Demonstrate and repeat
Leg action is not circular	Demonstrate and assist as necessary

BREASTSTROKE: Legs

Supine position with a woggle held under the arms

Aim: to develop breaststroke leg kick in a supine position.

This allows the swimmer to see their own legs kicking. The woggle provides stability for the beginner and, with the swimmer in a supine position, allows the teacher easy communication during the exercise.

Teacher's Focus
o Kick should be simultaneous
o Heels are drawn towards the seat
o The feet turn out just before the kick
o Feet kick back with knees just inline with the hips
o Feet come together at the end of the kick

Teaching Points
o Kick with both legs at the same time
o Keep your feet in the water
o Kick like a frog
o Kick and glide
o Point your toes at the end of the kick

Heels drive back in a circular whip like action giving the kick power and motion

Kick finishes in a streamlined position with legs straight and toes pointed

Common Faults	Corrective Practice
Feet are coming out of the water	Reiterate the teaching point and repeat
Failing to bring the heels up to the bottom	Repeat previous leg practice
Leg kick is not simultaneous	Reiterate teaching point and repeat
Legs are not straight at the end of the kick	Demonstrate and repeat

BREASTSTROKE: Legs

Static practice holding the poolside

Aim: to practise breaststroke leg action in a static position.

This allows the swimmer to develop correct technique in a prone position in the water. Kicking WITHOUT force and power should be encouraged during this exercise to avoid undue impact on the lower back.

Teacher's Focus
o Legs should be a mirror image
o Heels are drawn towards the seat
o The feet turn out just before the kick
o Feet kick back with knees inline with the hips
o Feet come together at the end of the kick with legs straight and toes pointed

Teaching Points
o Kick both legs at the same time
o Kick like a frog
o Draw a circle with your heels
o Make sure your legs are straight at the end of the kick

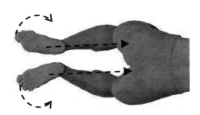

Heels drawn towards the seat and feet turn out

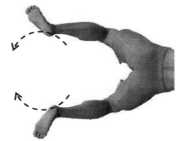

Heels draw round in a circular motion

Common Faults	Corrective Practice
Only turning one foot out	Repeat previous leg practices
Legs are not simultaneous	Reiterate the teaching point
Leg action is not circular	Repeat previous leg practices

BREASTSTROKE: Legs

Prone position with a float held under each arm

Aim: to practise and develop correct leg technique in a prone position.

Using two floats aids balance and stability and encourages correct body position whilst moving through the water.

Teacher's Focus
o Leg kick should be simultaneous
o Heels are drawn towards the seat
o The feet turn out just before the kick
o Feet kick back with knees inline with the hips
o Feet come together at the end of the kick

Teaching Points
o Keep your knees close together
o Point your toes to your shins
o Drive the water backwards with your heels
o Glide with legs straight at the end of the each kick

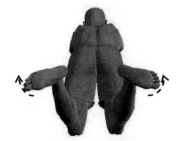
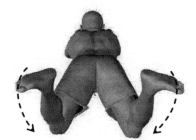

Heels are drawn up towards the seat. Soles face upwards

Feet turn outwards to allow the heels and soles to aid propulsion

Heels push back and outwards in a whip-like action

Common Faults	Corrective Practice
One foot turns out, causing a 'scissor' like kick	Repeat earlier leg practices
Legs kick back and forth	Reiterate the teaching point and repeat
Legs kick is not simultaneous	Reiterate the teaching point and repeat
Toes are not pointed at the end of the kick	Reiterate the teaching point and repeat

BREASTSTROKE: Legs

Holding a float out in front with both hands

Aim: to practise and learn correct kicking technique and develop leg strength.
Holding a single float or kickboard out in front isolates the legs and creates a slight resistance which demands a stronger kick with which to maintain momentum.

Teacher's Focus
o Kick should be simultaneous
o Legs drive back to provide momentum
o Heels are drawn towards the seat
o The feet turn out before the kick
o Feet come together at the end of the kick with legs straight and toes pointed

Teaching Points
o Drive the water backwards with force
o Turn your feet out and drive the water with your heels
o Kick and glide
o Kick like a frog
o Make your feet like a penguin

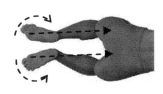

Heels drawn towards the seat and feet turn out

Heels drive back in a circular whip like action giving the kick power and motion

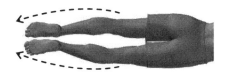

Kick finishes in a streamlined position with legs straight and toes pointed

Common Faults	Corrective Practice
Kick is slow and lacking power	Repeat earlier leg practices
Failing to bring the heels up to the bottom	Repeat earlier leg practices
Feet are breaking the water surface	Check the body position and repeat
Toes are not pointed at the end of the kick	Reiterate the teaching point and repeat

BREASTSTROKE: Legs

Arms stretched out in front holding a float vertically

Aim: to develop leg kick strength and power.

The float held vertically adds resistance to the movement and requires the swimmer to kick with greater effort. Ideal for swimmers with a weak leg kick.

Teacher's Focus

o Arms should be straight and float should be held partly underwater
o Kick should be a whip like action
o Feet kick back with knees inline with the hips
o Feet come together at the end of the kick

Teaching Points

o Kick your legs simultaneously
o Push the water with your heels and the soles of your feet
o Drive the water backwards with your heels

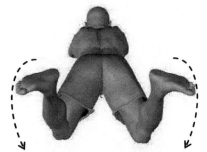

Heels push back and outwards in a whip-like action

Heels drive back to add power to the kick

Common Faults	Corrective Practice
Float is held flat or out of the water	Demonstrate and repeat
Not turning both feet out	Repeat earlier leg practices
Leg kick lacks sufficient power	Repeat earlier leg practices

BREASTSTROKE: Legs

Supine position with hands held on hips

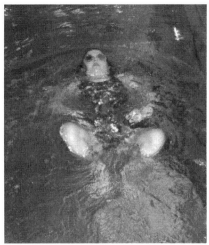

Aim: to develop leg kick strength and stamina.
This exercise is more advanced and requires the leg kick to be previously well practised.

Teacher's Focus
o Kick should be simultaneous
o Heels are drawn towards the seat
o The feet turn out just before the kick
o Feet kick back with knees inline with the hips
o Feet come together at the end of the kick
   with legs straight and toes pointed

Teaching Points
o Keep your feet in the water
o Kick like a frog
o Make sure your legs are straight after
   each kick
o Kick and glide
o Point your toes at the end of the kick

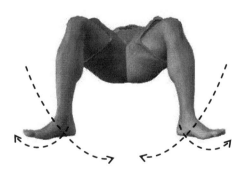

Feet turn out as the legs begin to kick round in a circular action

Common Faults	Corrective Practice
Not turning both feet out	Reiterate the teaching point
Kick is not hard enough to provide power	Repeat the previous leg practice
Legs are not straight at the end of the kick	Reiterate the teaching point and repeat
Toes are not pointed at the end of the kick	Reiterate the teaching point and repeat

BREASTSTROKE: Legs

Moving practice with arms stretched out in front

Aim: to practise correct kicking technique and develop leg strength

This is an advanced exercise as holding the arms out in front demands a stronger kick with which to maintain momentum whilst maintaining a streamlined body position.

Teacher's Focus
- o Kick should be simultaneous
- o The feet turn out just before the kick
- o Feet kick back with knees just inline with the hips
- o Feet come together at the end of the kick with legs straight and toes pointed

Teaching Points
- o Keep your knees close together
- o Drive the water with your heels
- o Make sure your legs are straight at the end of the kick
- o Kick and glide

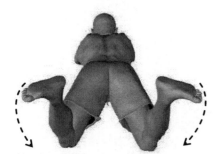

Heels push back and outwards in a whip-like action

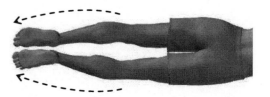

Kick finishes in a streamlined position with legs straight and toes pointed

Common Faults	Corrective Practice
Not turning both feet out	Reiterate the teaching point
Feet are breaking the water surface	Check the body position and repeat
Legs are not straight at the end of the kick	Repeat earlier leg practices
Toes are not pointed at the end of the kick	Repeat earlier leg practices

BREASTSTROKE: Arms

Static practice standing on the poolside

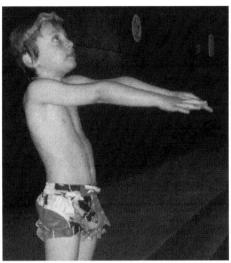
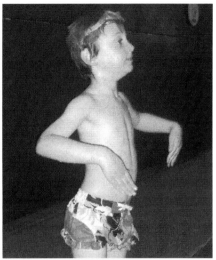

Aim: to learn the arm pull technique in its most basic form.

On the pool side, either sitting or standing, the swimmer can practise and perfect the movement without the resistance of the water.

Teacher's Focus
- o Arm action should be simultaneous
- o Fingers should be together
- o Arm pull should be circular
- o Elbows should be tucked in after each pull
- o Arms should extend forward and together after each pull

Teaching Points
- o Both arms pull at the same time
- o Keep your fingers closed together
- o Keep your hands flat
- o Tuck your elbows into your sides after each pull
- o Stretch your arms forward until they are straight
- o Draw an upside down heart with your hands

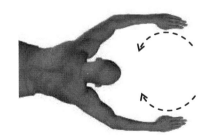

Arms and hands pull around and downwards

Elbows tuck in and arms extend forward

Common Faults	Corrective Practice
Fingers apart	Reiterate the teaching point and repeat
Arms pull at different speeds	Demonstrate and repeat
Arms pull past the shoulders	Demonstrate and repeat
Elbows fail to tuck in each time	Reiterate the teaching point and repeat
Arms fail to extend full forward	Demonstrate and repeat

BREASTSTROKE: Arms

Walking practice moving through shallow water

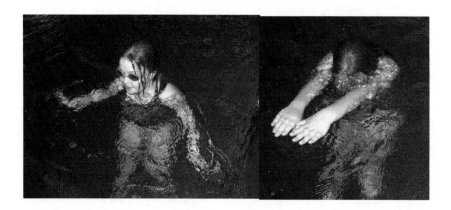

Aim: to practise and develop correct arm technique from in the water.

The swimmer can experience the feel of pulling the water whilst walking along the pool floor. Where the water is too deep, this exercise can be performed standing on the poolside. Submerging the face is optional at this stage.

Teacher's Focus
o Arm action should be simultaneous
o Arms and hands should remain under water
o Fingers should be together
o Arms should extend forward and together until straight after each pull

Teaching Points
o Pull with both arms at the same time
o Keep your hands under the water
o Tuck your elbows into your sides after each pull
o Stretch your arms forward until they are straight
o Draw an upside down heart with your hands

Arms and hands pull back in a
circular motion

Elbows tuck in and arms and hands stretch forward into a glide

Common Faults	Corrective Practice
Fingers are apart	Reiterate the teaching point and repeat
Arms pull past the shoulders	Demonstrate and repeat
Elbows fail to tuck in each time	Demonstrate and repeat
Arms fail to extend full forward	Reiterate the teaching point and repeat
Hands come out of the water	Reiterate the teaching point and repeat

BREASTSTROKE: Arms

Moving practice with a woggle held under the arms

Aim: to learn correct arm action whilst moving through the water.

The use of the woggle means that leg kicks are not required to assist motion and this then helps develop strength in the arm pull. The woggle slightly restricts arm action but not enough to negate the benefits of this exercise.

Teacher's Focus
- Arm action should be simultaneous
- Arms and hands should remain under water
- Arms and hands should extend forward after the pull
- Fingers should be together
- Arm pull should be circular

Teaching Points
- Pull round in a circle
- Keep your hands under the water
- Keep your fingers together and hands flat
- Pull your body through the water
- Draw an upside down heart with your hands

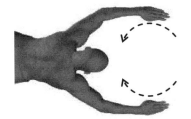
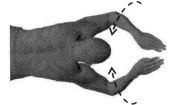

Arms and hands pull around and downwards

Elbows tuck in and arms and hands stretch forward into a glide

Common Faults	Corrective Practice
Fingers are apart	Repeat earlier arm practices
Arms fail to extend fully forward	Demonstrate and repeat
Hands come out of the water	Reiterate the teaching point and repeat
Arms extend forward too far apart	Reiterate the teaching point and repeat

BREASTSTROKE: Arms

Arms only with a pull-buoy held between the legs

Aim: to develop strength in the arm pull.

The pull-buoy prevents the legs from kicking, therefore isolating the arms. As the legs are stationary, forward propulsion and a glide action is difficult and therefore the arm action is made stronger as it has to provide all the propulsion for this exercise.

Teacher's Focus
o Arms and hands should remain under water
o Arm pull should be circular
o Elbows should be tucked in after each pull
o Arms should extend forward and together

Teaching Points
o Keep your hands under the water
o Pull your body through the water
o Keep your elbows high as you pull
o Tuck your elbows into your sides after each pull
o Stretch your arms forward until they are straight

Arms and hands pull back in a
circular motion

Elbows tuck in and arms and hands stretch
forward together

Common Faults	Corrective Practice
Arms pull past the shoulders	Demonstrate and repeat
Elbows fail to tuck in each time	Repeat earlier arm practices
Arms fail to extend full forward	Reiterate the teaching point and repeat
Hands come out of the water	Repeat earlier arm practices
Arms extend forward too far apart	Demonstrate and repeat

BREASTSTROKE: Arms

Push and glide adding arm pulls

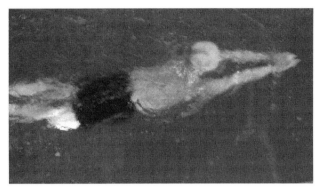

Aim: to progress arm action and technique from previous exercises

By incorporating a push and glide, this allows the swimmer to practise maintaining a correct body position whilst using the arms. This is a more advanced exercise as the number of arms pulls and distance travelled will vary according to the strength of the swimmer.

Teacher's Focus
o Arms and hands should remain under water
o Elbows should be tucked in after each pull
o Arms should extend forward into a glide position
o Body position should be maintained throughout

Teaching Points
o Keep your hands under the water
o Pull your body through the water
o Tuck your elbows into your sides after each pull
o Stretch your arms forward with hands together

Direction of travel →

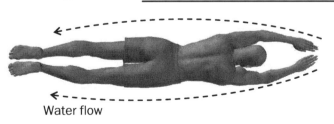

Water flow

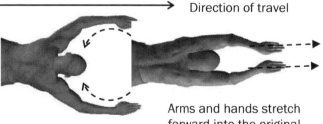

Arms and hands pull around and downwards

Arms and hands stretch forward into the original glide position

Common Faults	Corrective Practice
Arms pull past the shoulders	Repeat earlier arm practices
Arms fail to extend full forward	Demonstrate and repeat
Hands come out of the water	Repeat earlier arm practices
Arms extend forward too far apart	Reiterate the teaching point and repeat
Arms fail to bend during the pull	Repeat earlier arm practices

BREASTSTROKE: Breathing

Static practice, breathing with arm action

Aim: to practise breast stroke breathing action whilst standing in the water.
This allows the swimmer to experience the feel of breathing into the water in time with the arm action, without the need to actually swim.

Teacher's Focus
- o Breath inwards at the end of the in sweep
- o Head lifts up as the arms complete the pull
- o Head should clear the water
- o Head returns to the water as the arms recover
- o Breath out is as the hands recover forward

Teaching Points
- o Breathe in as you complete your arm pull
- o Breathe out as your hands stretch forwards
- o Blow your hands forwards

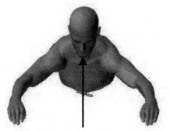

Breathe IN as the arms pull
down and the head rises

Breathe OUT as the arms recover forward
and the face enters the water

Common Faults	Corrective Practice
Head fails to clear the water	Demonstrate and repeat
Breathing out as the arms pull back	Reiterate the teaching point and repeat
Lifting the head to breathe as the arms recover	Reiterate the teaching point and repeat

BREASTSTROKE: Breathing

Breathing practice with woggle under the arms

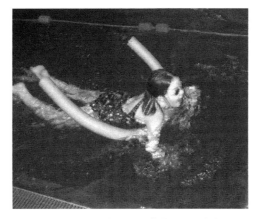

Aim: to develop correct synchronisation of breathing and arm pull technique.

The woggle provides support which enables the exercise to be done slowly at first. It also allows the swimmer to travel during the practice. Leg action can be added if necessary.

Note: the woggle can restrict complete arm action.

Teacher's Focus
- Breath inwards at the end of the in-sweep
- Head lifts up as the arms complete the pull back
- Head should clear the water
- Head returns to the water as the arms recover
- Breathing out is as the hands stretch forward

Teaching Points
- Breathe in as you complete your arm pull
- Breathe out as your hands stretch forwards
- Blow your hands forwards

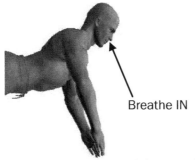

Breathe IN

Breathing in occurs as the arms pull down and the head rises above the surface

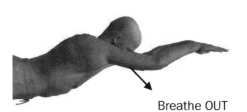

Breathe OUT

Breathing out occurs as the arms recover out in front

Common Faults	Corrective Practice
Holding the breath	Repeat earlier breathing practices
Head fails to clear the water	Repeat previous breathing practices
Breathing out as the arms pull back	Repeat previous breathing practices
Lifting the head as the arms stretch forward	Reiterate the teaching point and repeat

BREASTSTROKE: Breathing

Float held in front, breathing with leg kick

Aim: to develop the breathing technique in time with the leg kick.

The float provides stability and allows the swimmer to focus on the breathe kick glide action.

Teacher's Focus
o Inward breathing should be just before the knees bend
o Head lifts up as the knees bend ready to kick
o Mouth should clear the water
o Head returns to the water as the legs thrust backwards
o Breathe out is as the legs kick into a glide

Teaching Points
o Breathe in as your legs bend ready to kick
o Breathe out as you kick and glide
o Kick your head down

Breathe IN just before the knees bend for the kick

Breathe OUT as the legs kick into a glide

Common Faults	Corrective Practice
Holding the breath	Repeat earlier breathing practices
Head fails to clear the water	Repeat previous breathing practices
Breathing out as the knees bend ready to kick	Reiterate the teaching point and repeat
Lifting the head as the legs kick into a glide	Reiterate the teaching point and repeat

BREASTSTROKE: Timing

Slow practice with woggle under the arms

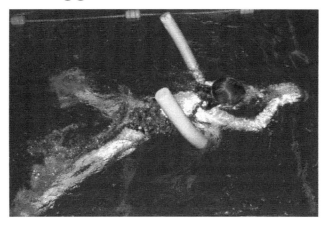

Aim: to practise the stroke timing in its most basic form.

The use of the woggle placed under the arms allows the swimmer to practice the exercise in stages as slowly as they need. It must be noted that the woggle resists against the glide and therefore the emphasis must be placed on the timing of the arms and legs. The glide can be developed using other exercises.

Teacher's Focus
o From a streamlined position arms should pull first
o Legs should kick into a glide
o Legs should kick as the hands and arms recover
o A glide should precede the next arm pull

Teaching Points
o Pull with your hands first
o Kick your hands forwards
o Kick your body into a glide
o Pull, breathe, kick, glide

Body position starts with hands and feet together

Pull, breathe, kick, glide sequence is performed

Swimmer returns to original body position.

Common Faults	Corrective Practice
Kicking and pulling at the same time	Demonstrate and repeat
Failure to glide	Reiterate the teaching point and repeat
Legs kick whilst gliding	Reiterate the teaching point and repeat

BREASTSTROKE: Timing

Push and glide, adding stroke cycles

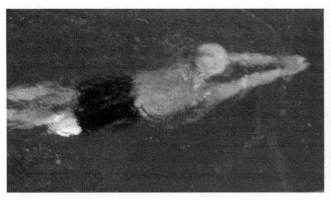 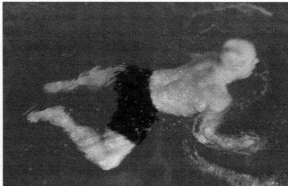

Aim: to practise and develop correct stroke timing.

The swimmer starts with a push and glide to establish a streamlined glide. The arm pull, breath in and then leg kick is executed in the correct sequence, resulting in another streamlined glide.

Teacher's Focus
o From a streamlined position arms should pull first
o Legs should kick into a glide
o Legs should kick as the hands and arms recover
o A glide should precede the next arm pull

Teaching Points
o Kick your hands forwards
o Kick your body into a glide
o Pull, breathe, kick, glide

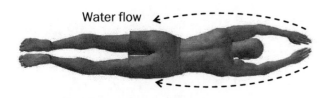

Push and glide to establish body position

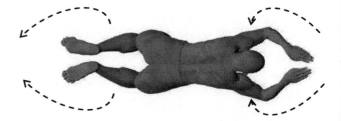

Pull, breathe, kick and glide again

Common Faults	Corrective Practice
Kicking and pulling at the same time	Repeat previous timing practice
Failure to glide	Reiterate the teaching point and repeat
Legs kick whilst gliding	Reiterate the teaching point and repeat

BREASTSTROKE: Timing

Two kicks, one arm pull

Aim: to perfect timing whilst maintaining a streamlined body position.

From a push and glide, the swimmer performs a 'pull, breathe, kick, glide' stroke cycle into another streamlined glide. They then perform an additional kick whilst keeping the hands and arms stretched out in front. This encourages concentration on timing and coordination and at the same time develops leg kick strength.

Teacher's Focus

o Legs should kick into a glide
o Legs should kick as the hands and arms recover
o A glide should follow each leg kick
o Head lifts to breath with each arm pull

Teaching Points

o Kick your body into a glide
o Pull, breathe, kick, glide

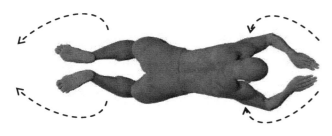

A full stroke cycle is performed from a push and glide

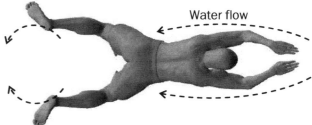

Additional kick whilst the hands and arms remain still

Common Faults	Corrective Practice
Arms pull too often and too early	Demonstrate and repeat
Failure to glide	Repeat earlier timing practices
Failure to keep the hands together for the second kick	Demonstrate and repeat

BREASTSTROKE: Full Stroke

Full stroke

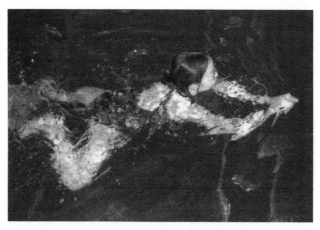

Aim: to swim full stroke Breast Stroke demonstrating efficient arm and leg action, with regular breathing and correct timing.

Teacher's Focus
o Head remains still and central
o Shoulders remain level
o Leg kick is simultaneous
o Feet turn out and drive backwards
o Arm action should be circular and simultaneous
o Breathing is regular with each stroke cycle

Teaching Points
o Kick and glide
o Kick your hands forwards
o Drive your feet backward through the water
o Keep your fingers together and under the water
o Pull in a small circle then stretch forward
o Breath with each stroke

Heels draw up towards the seat and feet turn out

Arms pull in a circular action and elbows tuck in

Legs kick backwards providing power and propulsion

Arms stretch forward into a glide

Common Faults	Corrective Practice
Failure to glide	Repeat earlier timing practices
Stroke is rushed	Encourage a longer glide and repeat
Leg kick is not simultaneous	Repeat earlier leg practices
Arms pull to the sides	Repeat earlier arm practices
Failing to breath regularly	Repeat earlier breathing practices

Breaststroke

Exercise quick reference guide

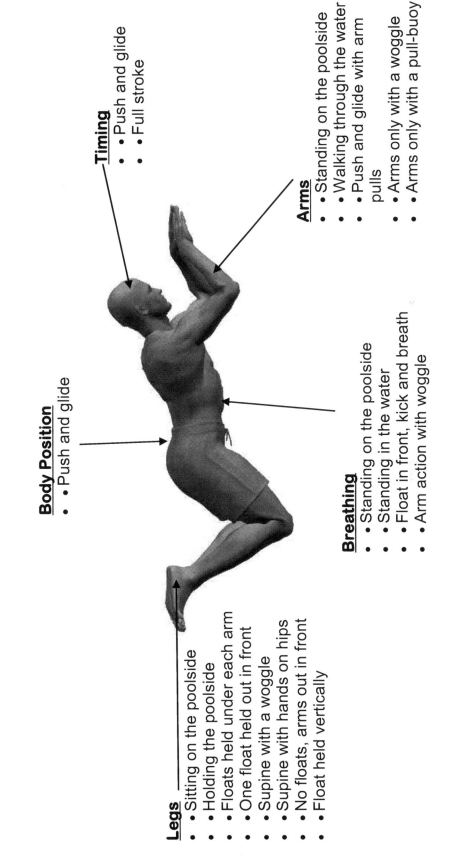

Timing
- • Push and glide
- • Full stroke

Arms
- • Standing on the poolside
- • Walking through the water
- • Push and glide with arm pulls
- • Arms only with a woggle
- • Arms only with a pull-buoy

Body Position
- • Push and glide

Breathing
- • Standing on the poolside
- • Standing in the water
- • Float in front, kick and breath
- • Arm action with woggle

Legs
- • Sitting on the poolside
- • Holding the poolside
- • Floats held under each arm
- • One float held out in front
- • Supine with a woggle
- • Supine with hands on hips
- • No floats, arms out in front
- • Float held vertically

Stroke Practices

Butterfly

BUTTERFLY: Body Position

Holding the poolside

Aim: to practise the body position and movement by holding on to the poolside.
The swimmer performs an undulating action whilst using the poolside or rail for support.
Note: this exercise should be performed slowly and without force or power as the static nature places pressure on the lower back.

Teacher's Focus
o Exercise should be slow and gradual
o Head remains central
o Shoulders and hips should be level
o Horizontal body with an undulating movement
o Wave like movement from head to toe
o Legs remain together

Teaching Points
o Keep your head in the middle
o Make the top of your head lead first
o Keep your shoulders level
o Keep your hips level
o Make your body into a long wave

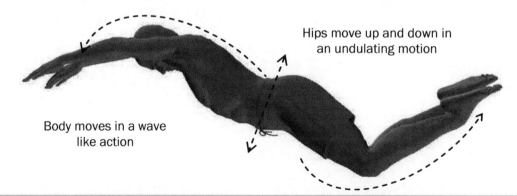

Hips move up and down in an undulating motion

Body moves in a wave like action

Common Faults	Corrective Practice
Body remains too stiff and rigid	Encourage the pupil to relax and repeat
Head moves to the sides	Reiterate the teaching point
Shoulders and hips are not remaining level	Demonstrate and repeat

BUTTERFLY: Body Position

Dolphin dives

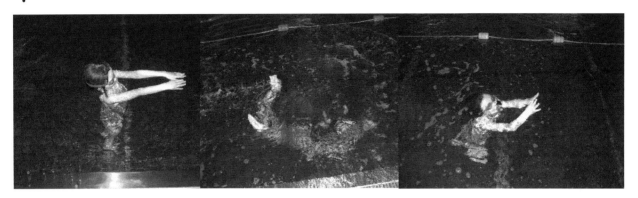

Aim: to develop an undulating body movement whilst travelling through water of standing depth.

The swimmer performs a series of dives from a standing position, diving deep under the surface, arching the back and resurfacing immediately to stand up. The aim is to perform as many dolphin dives across the width as possible. Pupils can then progress to performing the practice without standing in-between dives.

Teacher's Focus
- Head remains central
- Shoulders and hips should be level
- Body moves with an undulating movement
- Wave-like movement from head to toe
- Legs remain together

Teaching Points
- Keep your head in the middle
- Make the top of your head dive down first
- Make your body into a huge wave
- Stretch up to the surface

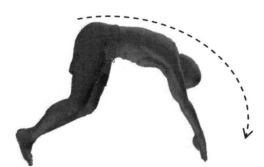 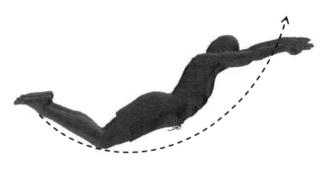

Body dives down and then resurfaces immediately in a wave like movement

Common Faults	Corrective Practice
Body remains too stiff and rigid	Encourage movement to flow
Body dives but fails to undulate upwards	Reiterate the teaching point
Leading with the head looking forwards	Encourage the pupil to focus downwards

BUTTERFLY: Body Position

Push and glide

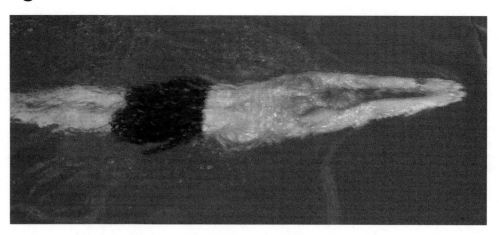

Aim: to practise and develop an undulating whilst moving.

The swimmer pushes from the poolside into a glide and then begins the undulating action from head to toe. This allows the swimmer to experience the required undulating action whilst moving through the water.

Teacher's Focus
- Head remains central
- Shoulders and hips should be level
- Body is horizontal with an undulating movement
- Wave-like movement from head to toe
- Legs remain together

Teaching Points
- Make the top of your head lead first
- Keep your shoulders level
- Keep your hips level
- Make your body into a long wave
- Pretend you are a dolphin swimming

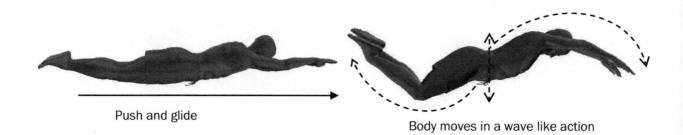

Push and glide

Body moves in a wave like action

Common Faults	Corrective Practice
Body remains too stiff and rigid	Encourage the pupil to relax and repeat
Shoulders and hips are not remaining level	Repeat earlier body position practices
Leading with the head looking forwards	Encourage the pupil to look downwards

BUTTERFLY: Legs

Sitting on the poolside

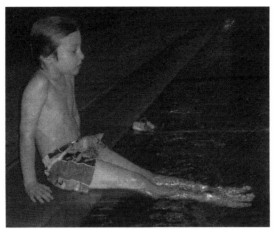

Aim: to develop the kicking action whilst sitting on the poolside.
Bending and kicking from the knees with legs together allows the swimmer to practise the correct movement and feel the water at the same time.

Teacher's Focus
o Simultaneous legs action
o Knees bend and kick in upbeat to provide propulsion
o Legs accelerate on upbeat
o Toes are pointed

Teaching Points
o Kick both legs at the same time
o Keep your ankles loose
o Keep your legs together
o Point your toes

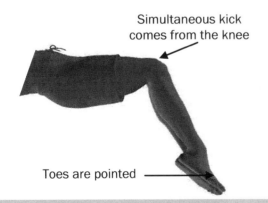

Simultaneous kick comes from the knee

Toes are pointed

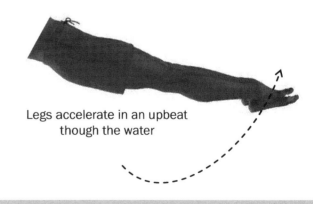

Legs accelerate in an upbeat though the water

Common Faults	Corrective Practice
Leg kick is not simultaneous	Reiterate the teaching point and practice
Toes are not pointed	Demonstrate and repeat
Overall action is too stiff and rigid	Encourage the pupil to relax and repeat
Kick is not deep or powerful enough	Reiterate the need for a powerful kick

BUTTERFLY: Legs

Push and glide adding leg kick

Aim: to practise the dolphin leg kick action and experience movement.
This allows the swimmer the develop propulsion from the accelerating leg kick and undulating body movement.

Teacher's Focus
o Simultaneous legs action
o Knees bend and kick in downbeat to provide propulsion
o Legs accelerate on downbeat
o Toes are pointed
o Hips initiate undulating movement

Teaching Points
o Keep your ankles loose
o Kick downwards powerfully
o Keep your legs together
o Point your toes
o Kick like a mermaid

Simultaneous kick comes from the knee

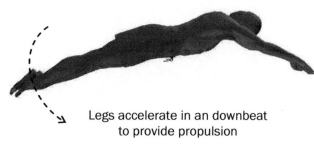

Legs accelerate in an downbeat to provide propulsion

Common Faults	Corrective Practice
Leg kick is not simultaneous	Reiterate the teaching point and repeat
Toes are not pointed	Reiterate the teaching point and repeat
Overall action is too stiff and rigid	Repeat the previous leg practice
Kick is not deep or powerful enough	Reiterate the teaching point and repeat

BUTTERFLY: Legs

Prone holding a float with both hands

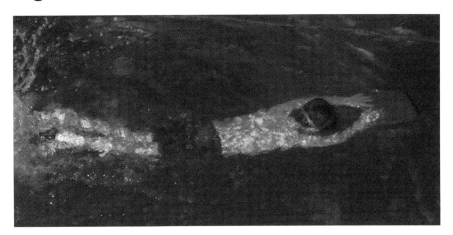

Aim: to develop the leg kick using a float for support.

This practice allows the advanced swimmer to develop leg kick strength and stamina as the float isolates the legs.

Teacher's Focus
- Simultaneous legs action
- Knees bend and kick in downbeat to provide propulsion
- Legs accelerate on downbeat
- Toes are pointed
- Hips initiate undulating movement

Teaching Points
- Kick both legs at the same time
- Kick downwards powerfully
- Keep your legs together
- Make your body into a huge wave
- Pretend you are swimming like a mermaid

Powerful leg kick provides propulsion and help the body to undulate

Common Faults	Corrective Practice
Leg kick is not simultaneous	Repeat earlier leg practices
Toes are not pointed	Repeat earlier leg practices
Overall action is too stiff and rigid	Encourage the pupil to relax and repeat
Kick is not deep or powerful enough	Reiterate teaching point and repeat

BUTTERFLY: Legs

Supine position with arms by sides

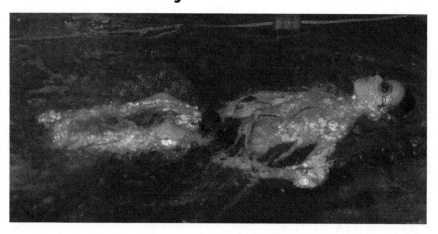

Aim: to practise and develop a dolphin leg kick in a supine position.
This allows the swimmer to kick continuously whilst facing upwards. This practice requires a great deal of leg strength and stamina and therefore is ideal for developing these aspects of the stroke.

Teacher's Focus
o Simultaneous legs action
o Knees bend and kick in upbeat to provide propulsion
o Legs accelerate on upbeat
o Toes are pointed
o Hips initiate undulating movement

Teaching Points
o Kick both legs at the same time
o Keep your ankles loose
o Kick upwards powerfully
o Keep your legs together
o Point your toes

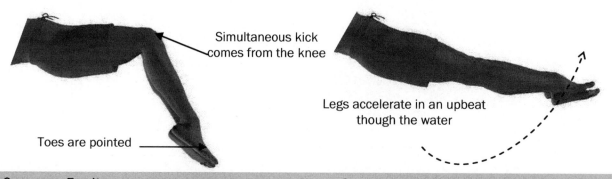

Simultaneous kick comes from the knee

Toes are pointed

Legs accelerate in an upbeat though the water

Common Faults	Corrective Practice
Leg kick is not simultaneous	Repeat earlier leg practices
Overall action is too stiff and rigid	Repeat earlier leg practices
Hips are not undulating to initiate the kick	Repeat previous leg practice
Kick is not deep or powerful enough	Repeat earlier leg practices

BUTTERFLY: Legs

Kick and roll

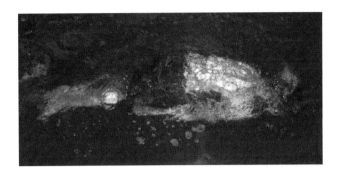 

Aim: to combine the leg kick and undulating body movement and perform a rolling motion through the water.

This practice can be performed with arms held by the sides or held out in front. The rolling motion forces the swimmer to use the head, shoulders and hips to produce the movement required for powerful undulating propulsion.

Teacher's Focus
o Simultaneous legs action
o Head and shoulders initiate rolling motion
o Knees bend and kick to provide propulsion
o Legs accelerate on downbeat
o Hips initiate undulating movement

Teaching Points
o Kick both legs at the same time
o Keep your ankles loose
o Roll like a cork screw
o Keep your legs together
o Make your body snake through the water

Legs kick and body performs a 'cork screw' like roll through the water

Common Faults	Corrective Practice
Leg kick is not simultaneous	Repeat earlier leg practices
Overall action is too stiff and rigid	Reiterate the teaching point and repeat
Kick is not powerful enough	Repeat earlier leg practices

BUTTERFLY: Arms

Standing on the poolside

 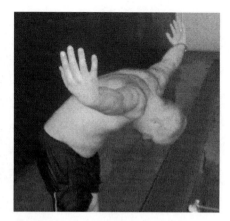

Aim: to practise correct butterfly arm action whilst standing on the poolside.
The pupil is able to work through the arm action slowly and in stages so as to experience the basic movement required.

Teacher's Focus
o Arms move simultaneously
o Hands enter the water in line with the shoulders
o Hands pull in the shape of a keyhole
o Hands push past the thigh

Teaching Points
o Move both arms at the same time
o Thumbs go in first
o Draw a keyhole under your body
o Push past your thighs

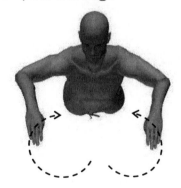

Arms pull through in a keyhole shape

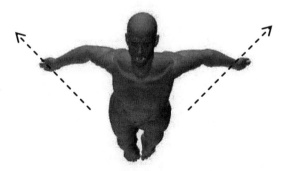

Arms pull through and past the thighs

Common Faults	Corrective Practice
Arm action is not simultaneous	Reiterate the teaching point and repeat
Arms are too straight	Encourage elbow bend and repeat
Arms are not pulling back to the thighs	Reiterate the teaching point and repeat

BUTTERFLY: Arms

Walking on the pool floor

Aim: to progress from the previous practice and develop the arm action.

The swimmer can get a feel for the water whilst walking and performing the simultaneous arm action.

Teacher's Focus

o Arms move simultaneously
o Hands enter the water in line with the shoulders
o Hands pull in the shape of a keyhole
o Hands push past the thigh

Teaching Points

o Move both arms at the same time
o Thumbs go in first
o Draw a keyhole under your body
o Push past your thighs

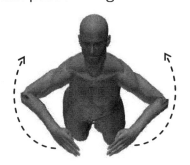

Arms pull through simultaneously

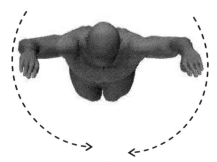

Arms are thrown forwards over the water surface

Common Faults	Corrective Practice
Arm action is not simultaneous	Repeat previous arm practice
Arms are too straight	Demonstrate and repeat
Fingers are apart	Reiterate the teaching point and repeat
Hands fail to clear the water	Reiterate the teaching point and repeat

BUTTERFLY: Arms

Push and glide adding arms

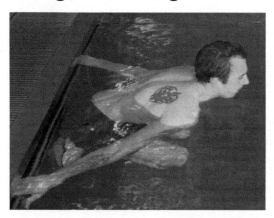 

Aim: to practise the arm action whilst moving through the water.

Correct body position is established from the push and glide and the swimmer can then use the arm action to maintain momentum through the water. A limited number of arm pulls can be achieved with this practice.

Teacher's Focus
- Arms move simultaneously
- Fingers closed together
- Thumbs enter the water first
- Hands enter the water in line with the shoulders
- Hands push past the thigh
- Hands clear water surface on recovery

Teaching Points
- Move both arms at the same time
- Thumbs enter water first
- Pull hard through the water
- Pull past your thighs
- Throw your arms over the water

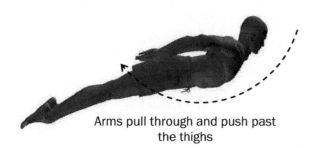

Arms pull through and push past the thighs

Arms recover over the water surface

Common Faults	Corrective Practice
Arms are too straight	Demonstrate and repeat
Arms are not pulling back to the thighs	Reiterate the teaching point and repeat
Hands fail to clear the water	Reiterate the teaching point and repeat

BUTTERFLY: Arms

Arms only using a pull-buoy

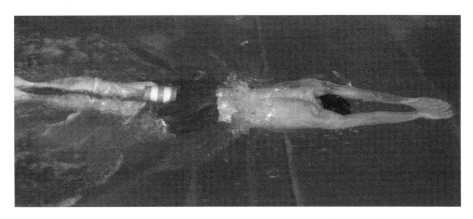

Aim: to help the swimmer develop arm strength and stamina.

This practice is performed over a longer distance, progressing from the previous practice. The pull buoy provides buoyancy and support as well as help the undulating body movement.

Teacher's Focus
◊ Arms move simultaneously
◊ Fingers closed together
◊ Thumbs enter the water first
◊ Hands enter the water in line with the shoulders
◊ Hands push past the thigh
◊ Hands clear water surface on recovery

Teaching Points
o Thumbs go in first
o Pull hard through the water
o Pull past your thighs
o Throw your arms over the water

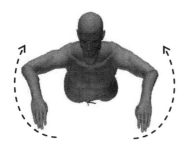

Arms pull through the water with power

Hands and arms clear the water on recovery

Common Faults	Corrective Practice
Arms are too straight	Demonstrate and repeat
Arms are not pulling back to the thighs	Repeat earlier arm practices
Hands fail to clear the water	Reiterate teaching point and repeat

BUTTERFLY: Arms

Arm action with breaststroke leg kicks

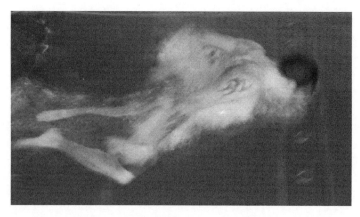

Aim: to enable use of breaststroke leg kicks to support the arm action.

As the legs kick, the propulsion helps the body to rise and the arms to recover over the water surface. This practice is also a good introduction to the timing of butterfly arms and legs.

Teacher's Focus
o Thumbs enter the water first
o Hands pull in the shape of a keyhole
o Hands push past the thigh
o Little finger exits the water first
o Hands clear water surface on recovery

Teaching Points
o Thumbs go in first
o Draw a keyhole under your body
o Pull past your thighs
o Little finger comes out first
o Throw your arms over the water

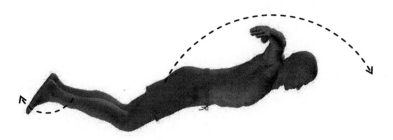

Leg kick helps the arms to recover over the water surface

Common Faults	Corrective Practice
Arms are too straight	Demonstrate and repeat
Arms are not pulling back to the thighs	Reiterate the teaching point and repeat
Fingers are apart	Reiterate the teaching point and repeat
Hands fail to clear the water	Reiterate the teaching point and repeat

BUTTERFLY: Breathing

Standing breathing, with arm pulls

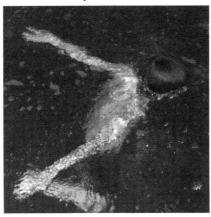

Aim: to incorporate butterfly breathing into the arm action.

This practice is performed standing either on the poolside or stationary in water of standing depth.

Teacher's Focus

- Breathing in should occur as the arms sweep up and out
- Explosive breathing is most beneficial
- Chin should remain in the water
- Face dives into the water as the arms come level with the shoulders
- Breath can be taken every stroke cycle or alternate cycles

Teaching Points

- Blow out hard as your chin rises
- Put your face down as your arms recover
- Push your chin forward and breathe every arm pull or every two arm pulls

Breathing occurs as the arms sweep up and out

Face submerges at the arms recover

Common Faults	Corrective Practice
Lifting the head too high	Demonstrate and repeat
Arms stop recovery to breathe	Encourage continuous arm action
Holding the breath	Reiterate the teaching point and repeat

BUTTERFLY: Breathing

Full stroke

Aim: to use the full stroke to practice breathing, incorporating regular breaths into the arm and leg actions.

Teacher's Focus
o Breathing in occurs as the arms sweep upwards
o Breathing in occurs as the legs are kicking downwards
o Explosive breathing is most beneficial
o Chin remains in the water
o Face dives into the water as the arms come level with the shoulders
o Breath can be taken every stroke cycle or alternate cycles

Teaching Points
o Blow out hard as your chin rises
o Lift your head to breathe in as your legs kick down
o Put your face down as your arms come over
o Push your chin forward and breathe every arm pull or every two arm pulls

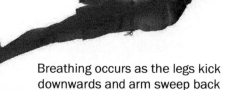

Breathing occurs as the legs kick downwards and arm sweep back

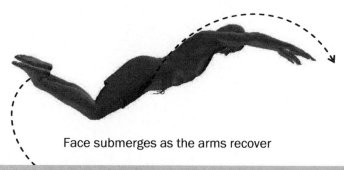

Face submerges as the arms recover

Common Faults	Corrective Practice
Lifting the head too high	Repeat previous breathing practice
Arms stop recovery to breathe	Repeat previous breathing practice
Holding the breath	Reiterate the teaching point and repeat
Breathing too often	Repeat previous breathing practice

BUTTERFLY: Timing

Full stroke

Aim: to perform the full stroke butterfly, incorporating two leg kicks per arm pull.

Teacher's Focus
- o Two legs kicks per arm cycle
- o Legs kick once as hands enter and sweep out
- o Legs kick once as arms sweep up and out

Teaching Points
- o Kick hard as your hands enter the water
- o Kick again as your hands pull under your body

Legs kick downwards as the hands catch and begin to pull

Legs kick again as the arms pull through to the thighs

Common Faults	Corrective Practice
Only kicking once per arm cycle	Reiterate the teaching point and repeat
Kicking too many times per arm cycle	Reiterate the teaching point and repeat

Butterfly

Exercise quick reference guide

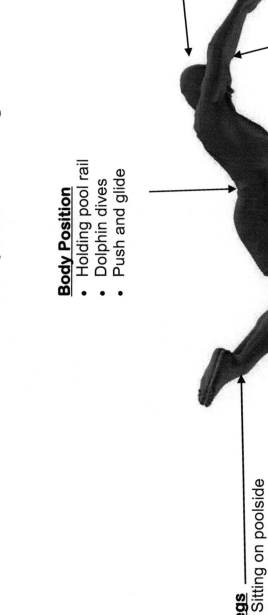

Body Position
- Holding pool rail
- Dolphin dives
- Push and glide

Timing
- Full stroke

Arms
- Standing on the poolside
- Walking through the water
- Push and glide, with arm pulls
- Arms only, with a pull-buoy
- Arm action with breaststroke legs

Breathing
- Standing breathing, with arm pulls
- Full stroke

Legs
- Sitting on poolside
- Float out in front
- Push and glide adding legs
- Supine arms by sides
- Kick and roll

Index of stroke practices

Front Crawl

Backstroke

Breaststroke

Butterfly

How to Be A Swimming Teacher

is available in FULL COLOUR as an eBook download

Download it online now from SWIM TEACH
www.swim-teach.com

Also available from all major eBook retailers

25180207R00083

Printed in Poland
by Amazon Fulfillment
Poland Sp. z o.o., Wrocław